RECIPES FROM THE CHATEAUX

Gilles and Bleuzen du Pontavice

Collection directed by
BLEUZEN DU PONTAVICE

Photographs
CLAUDE HERLÉDAN

TRANSLATION
DÉDICACE

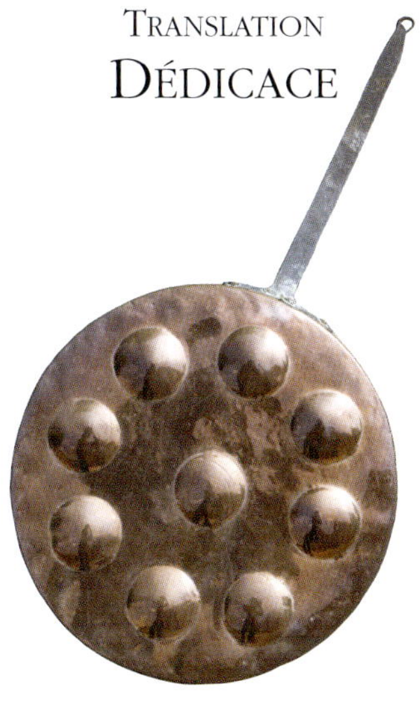

Editions OUEST-FRANCE

1646 : This region called Normandy is the most beautiful and the best province in France [...]. Its sky is mild and temperate, its soil joyful and fertile for all that is needed for subsistence and the delight of its inhabitants.»

It is thus that Eustache de Denneville, in his *Inventaire de l'Histoire de Normandie*, described the richest province in the kingdom which provided a quarter of its income. A fertile land, a much loved land, but, nonetheless, also an adventurous and scattered land.

Occupied at the start of our era by numerous tribes, Normandy was unified by the Treaty of Saint-Clair-sur-Epte, becoming a market entrusted to Rollon, one of its so-called «Norman» invaders, who became the Province's first Duke. His companions, with those from Harcourt at the head, formed the basis for the old Norman nobility who, often, made their names during the crusades. In a daring expedition, the most famous of Rollon's successors, William the Conqueror, took the throne of England in 1066, a feat which is recounted in the famous Bayeux Tapestry. It was only natural that Normandy, now the master of England, barely concerned itself with fulfilling its vassalage links with the Kings of France, who, already, were finding it hard to control their kingdom!

Normandy has been completely French since Charles VII, although his enthronement was thanks to Joan of Arc, delivered to the English and burnt at the stake in Rouen. It is a province closer to Paris and more prosperous than any other, but the call of the open sea and of the capital drained it of its population and it is only recently that new roads have connected it properly to the North and to Brittany.

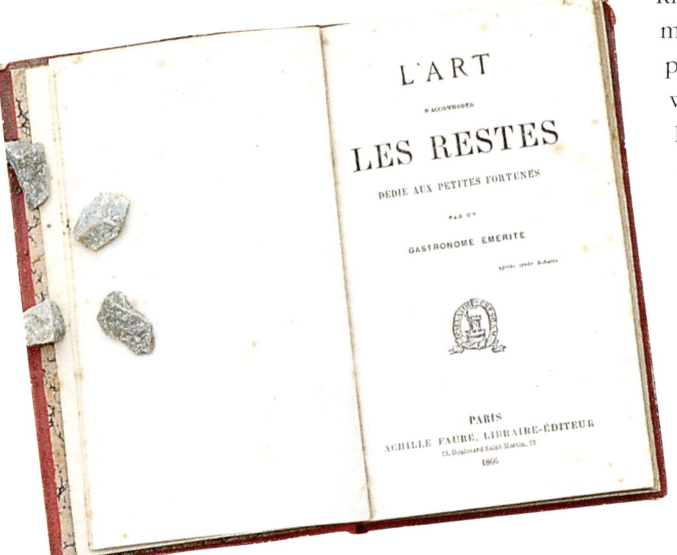

L'ART

D'ACCOMMODER

LES RESTES

DÉDIÉ AUX PETITES FORTUNES

PAR UN

GASTRONOME ÉMÉRITE

PARIS

ACHILLE FAURE, LIBRAIRE-ÉDITEUR

23, Boulevard Saint-Martin, 23

1866

Knowing how to use leftovers is the basis of rural cusine. Here, a small recipe book for the cuisine of Sassy.

Rich fields and a bountiful dairy, Normandy is not the garden of France, but its pasture and cowshed. It is also maritime with good ports and the mouth of the River Seine which used to be the route to Paris. This is the reason for the scale of its fortresses, the most famous of which is Château-Gaillard. These buildings remind us that, for many long years, this land was the territory of soldiers until the Second World War saw the destruction of many towns and castles and scattered its coastline with the debris of battles. Normandy is also a reminder of these difficult times.

But, the Norman spirit has resisted. A spirit slightly coarse and cynical, with enough good sense to straighten the cliffs of Cauchois and the carrots of Créances! It is a land of writers, some of whom we will refer to in an indispensable « *Trou Normand* », well-rooted in the *bocage* and the *clos-masures*. A huge difference: far from Cotentin, erect against the winds, stand the salty polders of Mont-Saint-Michel and the green pastures of the Pays d'Auge – roughly the Basse-Normandie area - the more secretive Pays d'Ouche and the chequerboard of the Pays de Caux – roughly the Haute-Normandie area. Strangely, the province has formed two regions but during our research, we have found many common elements and, of course, a great love for this prosperous land and its good products, whether in large Louis XIII castles or small timber-framed manor houses. We would like to thank all those who opened their doors to us and allowed us to share in their cuisine and their recipe books.

At Château de Filieres. Superb products on a silver platter, this is châteaux cuisine.

MONUMENT HISTORIQUE

CROSVILLE

The watchman of Cotentin

From the top of the keep at Crosville, it is possible to see the marshes of Cotentin in the distance which give this land the appearance of a peninsula. Here, the English Channel does not have any clear boundaries and the fauna blends into the land and the sea. The castle bought by the Lefol family in 1985 was in a very poor state of repair and did not bear any signs of its noble past. This family had been the property's farmers for many years and Michèle Lefol, who grew up there, has undertaken a long renovation project.
Of an old castle there still remains some parts dating from the 15th century. The rest dates from the 17th century, in the severe style of Cotentin Louis XIII, both rural and agricultural, with a very attractive façade, simplified by a succession of triangular frontons pulled upwards by a projecting central pavilion. The staircase, with large granite steps, leads to the noble floor comprising several monumental items: beautiful fireplaces, polychrome decors depicting Ovid's «*Metamorphoses*».
The recipes entrusted to us by the Lefol family are very old, strongly marked by the terroir, but still topical. They are recipes of deceptive humility: the true cuisine of regions which knew how to make the most of its products. Furthermore, the castle also offers Norman meals and, every year, the Franco-British Plant Days provide a stepping-stone over the Channel.

A tall castle surmounted by a watchtower, protectedby its double gateway and its guard's tower, facing the Cotentin marshes.

MENU for the Norman Meal of 12 August

Pommeau
Chicken Broth with Tapioca
Chicken with Cider
Iron-baked Rice Pudding

This meal brought together dozens of guests in the castle's main hall with singers and storytellers from the region. The aperitif is Pommeau Normand, a traditional drink which has only been marketed in the past fifteen years. It is similar to Pineau but the grapes have been replaced with apples. It combines the strength of Calvados with the gentleness of fresh apple must. Pommeau should be drunk chilled beneath apple trees; it is also used a great deal in cooking for deglazing and seasoning dishes.

Chicken with Cider.

POULE AU CIDRE

Chicken with Cider

Farm-style chicken with firm and savoury flesh is indispensable.
If it weighs about 2kg, it is all the better. Cut it into small pieces and, if you find a few forming eggs inside, set them aside. Fry the chicken pieces in butter. Keep the bones to make chicken stock. Add a large chopped onion and brown it, sprinkle with flour and continue browning before adding a glass of Calvados and flambéing. Next, cover with 1 litre of cider (farm-style cider of course). Bring to the boil and reduce the heat. Add a bouqet garni, two sliced carrots and cover for 1 hour. Then, add a few peeled and quartered potatoes and the unformed eggs. Continue cooking for a further hour. Then, add two generous soupspoons of cream and stir gently. Serve this succulent dish with cider, the same one as used in the dish.

RIZ AU LAIT REPASSÉ

Iron-baked Rice Pudding

When « Salamandres » fast top-cooking grills did not exist, human ingenuity and good sense dictated creation.
The Devil takes Crèmes Brûlées!
Here, old-fashioned irons heated over a gas flame serve as « Salamandres ».

The rice pudding recipe is simple: 1 litre of milk, one cup of round rice, one cup of caster sugar, one sachet of vanilla sugar. Bring the milk to the boil and rinse the rice in cold running water and cook at a low heat for one hour. In the last 15 mins of cooking, add the sugar. Heat your well-cleaned iron on the stove. Place the rice in a bowl and sprinkle some brown sugar over the top. When the iron is very hot, place it carefully on top of the rice. Large clouds of sweet-smelling steam will be released and perfume everything around you. The heat from the iron forms a layer of glace, colourful sugar. Enjoy your meal!

Iron-Baked Rice Pudding.

Soupe à la graisse

Lard Soup

The lard is prepared with beef fat taken from around the kidneys. Melt it gently, without burning or colouring it, and add a variety of vegetables, parsley, laurel and thyme. Keep on a medium heat and cook under supervision for several days stirring the fat from time to time on the first day. Everything will darken in colour; care should be taken with this dish because the hot fat may spit and burn you!

Then, sieve the soup, press all the ingredients with the ladle, and remove the bone marrow and leave the perfumed and concentrated lard to cool. It may be kept for a very long time in earthenware jars. If you do not have the patience to make it yourself, you might be able to find it in very good delicatessens.

Next, to make lard soup, remove a piece of fat, place it in water with some garden vegetables and cook. When the soup is ready, place some biscuits (here well-cooked and browned unleavened bread) in the dish and cover with hot liquid. And, with that, you will be able to face the cold winter weather without fear.

Bouillie de sarrasin

Buckwheat Mixture

Take a bowl of buckwheat flour and stir gradually into 2 litres of cold milk and add coarse sea salt. Heat and stir until it has thickened. Season to taste. This mixture should be cooked the day before eating and left to cool in a baking tin. Cut into slices and cook on a buttered griddle or frying pan. Serve immediately.

We have found
a similar recipe in Brittany
which uses oat flour.

Sang-chaud

First recipe

Half a measure of milk and half a measure of blood, one chopped onion, pork kidney fat, salt, pepper. Two whisked eggs. Cook in a very hot oven. Similar to a soufflé.

Second recipe

White pudding and bard for one portion of cooked blood.

Heat adding milk, a little fresh cream and parley and season to taste. Simmer on a low heat. Stir well to equalise the quantities.

Back from Madame Lefol's garden. Crosville does not deny its status as an agricultural manor house.

Œufs au lait

Eggs cooked in milk

Measure out 125g of sugar, add to 1 litre of milk and bring to the boil. Add one vanilla pod split in half; whisk four eggs in a dish and gradually add the boiling milk stirring all the time after removing the vanilla pod. Pour into individual ramekins and cook in a bain-marie for 40 mins in an oven pre-heated at 220 °C. However, be sure to lower the temperature to 180 °C because the mixture must not boil or it will curdle and the dessert will be spoiled… well, maybe not completely spoiled but not as good as if it had been successful.

The fireplace in the Salle d'Apparat sums up Crosville: severe architecture, a desire for order reflected in the decorations on the small Corinthian columns but also two small vegetable gardens in the corner; daily life combined with formal life.

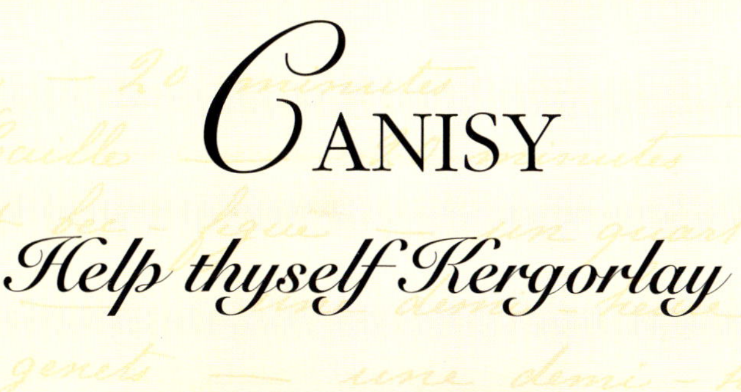

Canisy

Help thyself Kergorlay

Never sold, Canisy has been owned by the same family for the past thousand years. This old family from the interior of Brittany today receives guests at this large castle surrounded by lakes and an English-style park. The very first Lords, the sires of Carbonnel, have been known since the conquest of England by William the Conqueror. A tower still remains of a medieval castle which must have been a huge building with four wings. The other two towers form a large castle with bossing in red Troisgot stone, which gives the building its unity and monumental character. The architect was François Gabriel, the founder of a famous family line, who designed it for Hervé de Carbonnel. The only other two names in the history of the castle are Faudoas, the heir in the 18th century, and Kergolay, dating from 1787. Count Denis de Kergolay is the present owner. Canisy was damaged during the fighting which followed the D-Day Landings. Listed as a historic monument in 1945 it has since been restored and now plays host to seminars and meetings and even brides and grooms from the other side of the world.

Top.
Plaque on the fireplace with the Kergolay coat-of-arms: decorated in gold and gule. And the motto: « Help thyself Kergolay, God will help you. »
Opposite.
The fortified entrance to the Château of Canisy.

The recipes of Christian Small, the Head Chef at Château de Canisy

Poêlée de Saint-Jacques et langoustines aux arômes d'oranges et asperges vertes

Scallops and Dublin Bay Prawns with Orange and Green Asparagus Aromas

For 4 people
Preparation time: 30 mins
Cooking time: 10 mins
8 Scallops,
16 Dublin Bay Prawn Tails,
16 green asparagus,
200g of fresh spinach,
1 shallot,
1/2 bunch of chives,
3 freshly pressed oranges,
2cl of Grand-Marnier,
40g of butter,
4cl of olive oil,
salt, pepper,
a pinch of Espelette chilli pepper.

Remove the stalks and clean the spinach. Chop the shallot and the chives. Press the oranges. Peel and cook the asparagus for 4 mins (very al dente) and leave to cool.

Cut the scallops in two through the middle.

Cook the shallot with a small amount of butter, add the spinach leaves and cook for a few seconds. During this time, heat a frying pan with a small amount of olive oil and butter and brown the scallops for 30 seconds so that they stay pink on the inside. Keep warm.

Cook the Dublin bay prawns in the same way.

Add the Grand-Marnier and the orange juice and bring to the boil. Heat the asparagus in a small amount of water.

To dress the plates, place the spinach in the centre and lay the scallops and Dublin bay prawns on top. Place the strained asparagus around the outside of the plate and season the sauce, which should not be too thick. Add the chives and pour the sauce over the scallops and prawns. Serve very hot.

Scallops and Dublin Bay Prawns with Orange and Green Asparagus Aromas.

Duo de filets de bar et Matignon de légumes, sauce vierge

Duo of Sea Bass and Matignon of Vegetables with a Virgin Vauce

For 4 people
Preparation time: 1 hour.
Cooking time: 20 mins.
600g of sea bass fillets (4 fillets) cut in half,
4 chopped black olives,
olive oil,
salt, pepper.

Matignon of vegetables
100g of carrots,
100g of courgettes,
100g of mushrooms,
100g of peppers,
2cl of olive oil,
a few sprigs of tarragon,
1 sprigs of thyme.

Virgin sauce
400g of blanched tomatoes (peeled),
50g of shallots,
5cl of old wine vinegar,
5cl of olive oil,
1 teaspoon of crushed coriander seeds,
1 garlic clove,
1/2 teaspoon of tarragon,
1/2 teaspoon of basil.

To make the Matignon, wash and peel the vegetables and cut them into 2mm cubes. Brown the shallots in a little olive oil, add the diced carrots, cover and cook for 2 mins. Add the diced pepper and cook for 2 mins. Add the diced courgettes and cook for 2 mins and, finally, add the mushrooms, tarragon and thyme. Cook for a further 2 mins and place to the side.

To make the virgin sauce: remove the stalk bases from the tomatoes and cut the tops in the shape of a cross, place them in boiling water for a few seconds to remove the skin and cool them quickly in iced water, then peel and chop them. Mix with the chopped shallots and herbs, vinegar and olive oil. Season and place in the fridge.

Cut the sea bass fillets in half and place four pieces on greaseproof paper, large enough to be folded into small packets, and season. Place a small amount of the Matignon on each and cover with the second piece of sea bass.

Season again and close the paper. Place in an oven at 200 °C for about 10 mins.

During this time, heat the sauce without boiling it to retain the fresh taste of the tomatoes.

Open the papillottes and prepare the plates. Pour the sauce over the fish and serve very hot.

Duo of Sea Bass in front of a vase of Hemerocallis, daylily.

The castle was built in several stages, but the stone bonding has maintained its unity. Canisy, at the heart of a large rural estate, has a farm and its own vegetable garden which provides food for its table. It is an old story: in the middle of the 19th century, Hervé de Kergorlay turned his farm into a model establishment rewarded for its wheat yield and the quality of its cattle.

Sablé Marie-Victoire aux fruits rouges en gelée de vin

Marie-Victoire Shortbread Biscuit with Red Fruit and Wine Jelly

For 8 people
Preparation time: 1 hour
+ 5 hours in the fridge.
Cooking time: 15 mins.
250g of strawberries,
125g of raspberries,
125g of blackcurrants,
125g of bilberries or redcurrants,
250g of sugar,
zest of 1 lemon,
1 sprig of fresh mint,
1 bottle of red wine
(without too much tannin),
8 leaves of gelatine,
5cl of port,
1 sachet of green tea.
Shortbread biscuit
40g of egg yolks,
85g of sugar,
85g of half-salted butter,
130g of flour,
3g of baking powder,
25g of honey.

To make the dough, whisk the egg yolks and sugar and add the softened butter and honey. Add the flour and baking powder, mix with a spatula and place the dough in the fridge for 5 mins. Roll out with a small amount of flour and cut out discs the same size as the baking tin. Cook them at 160 °C on greaseproof paper for 12 to 15 mins. Remove from the tin once they have cooled. For the jellied fruit, wash and peel

the fruit, dry it and dice the strawberries. Soak the gelatine in very cold water. Pour the wine into a saucepan with the sugar and heat and flambé it. Once it has finished burning, extinguish the fire, add the strained gelatine and leave to melt. Add the sachet of tea and leave to infuse until it has cooled completely. Before the jelly sets, prepare a baking tin and line with film in order to facilitate removal. Place a layer of fruit in it and then pour the wine jelly up to the level of the fruit, leave to set for 15 mins, then add another layer of fruit and wine and leave to set again. Continue until all the ingredients have been used and leave to set in the fridge for 4 hours. To remove from the tin, first of all place a biscuit in the tin, then turn it out on to the serving dish and place a second biscuit on the top. Serve well chilled.

This dessert may be served with a little Chantilly cream.

The guest rooms bear names related to the castle's history: the Faudoas suite takes its name from one of the Kergorlay family's ancestors.

The castle's dining room is decorated with paintings of animals: the Lion and the Rat are reminiscent of La Fontaine and chickens decorate the fireplace.

Colombières

The gateway to Bessin

In the heart of Bessin, the Château de Colombières is the lovely offspring of a very ancient fortress. This can still be seen today, open on both sides, although it used to be enclosed by very high walls when it guarded the entrance to the interior of Normandy. The sea has ebbed since then, leaving a marsh which the Germans blocked in 1944 in order to impede the Allied landing.

A Colombières ancestor was a companion of William the Conqueror. The Bacon de Colombières family was replaced by the Bricqueville family, for whom the land was raised to the status of a marquessate. Since then, the castle has been passed on by succession and, today, is owned by Thérèse de Cosse-Brissac and her husband, Count Etienne de Maupeou d'Ableiges.

The fortified castle was altered in the 16th and 18th centuries: fewer defences, more light. Of the four corner towers, there now remain three, but a small octagonal tower has been set into the façade. Fortunately, the freshwater moat which surrounds the building is still there, giving it the appearance of a blessed island. Guests who stay there sleep in the old chapel and take their breakfast in a dining room overlooking the moat and the courtyard.

This kitchen which already existed in 1640 provided fire and water for the garrison. Although the well has since been blocked, the large fireplace and bread oven are still operational. On the table, a good Norman snack: Camembert, Livarot, Pont-l'Evêque and Colombières cider.

Menu of 14 october

Cheese Soufflé.

Cheese Soufflé
Beef with Carrots
Normandy Cheeses
Apple & Pear Crumble

Soufflé au fromage

Cheese Soufflé

Heat 50cl of milk and add salt and pepper. Make a roux with 40g of butter and 40g of flour. Add the milk and mix well. Add 200g of grated Gruyere cheese and five egg yolks. Mix well. Whisk six egg whites until stiff and add to the mixture.

Preheat the oven at 220 °C.

Butter a soufflé dish and pour in the mixture. Cook for 30 mins and watch closely.

Do not forget: «You wait for a soufflé, but a soufflé never waits».

Bœuf aux carottes

Beef with Carrots

Brown a piece of rump steak which has been coated with lard; add a little flour and cover with 50cl of white wine. Add some chopped onions, sliced carrots, quarters of turnip, a stick of celery, parsley and leave to cook at a low heat for 3 hours. One hour before the end, add some chanterelles or other mushrooms. Serve with roast potatoes.

Crumble pomme-poire

Apple & Pear Crumble

1kg of mixed fruit, 100g of flour, 100g of brown sugar and 100g of soft butter.

Rub the flour, sugar and butter together. Cut the fruit and lay in the oven dish and sprinkle with a little brown sugar.

Spread the crumble mix over the fruit and cook in the oven at a low heat for 1 hour.

Serve hot with thick cream diluted with a soupspoon of cold water.

Apple & Pear Crumble.

The levelling of the walls, which exceeded 10 metres, enabled Colombières to change from being an austere fortress to become a welcoming home which, nevertheless, does still retain evidence of its ancient status.

Menu

Feuillantine de Turbot

Dodine de Canard aux Raisins

Pommes en l'Air

et Jardinière fraîche de Légumes

Fromages

Charlotte de Fruits Rouges

Vins

Vins Blanc de Touraine

Riseccoli 1982

Tourte poireaux et saumon

Leek and Salmon Tart

Break the salmon, cooked in a court-bouillon, into small pieces. Cook the chopped leek. Cover the bottom of a pie dish with shortcrust pastry and add the well-drained leeks and salmon. Whisk a pot of cream with an egg and season well. Pour into the pie dish, cover with another layer of shortcrust pastry, seal and cut a hole in the centre. Mix an egg yolk with a little water and brush it over the pastry. Place in the oven and cook until the pastry is golden brown.

Pâté de foie de volaille

Chicken Liver Pate

Delicious on toast and served with an aperitif

Blend together 250g of chicken liver with the nerves removed, 500g of smoked pork belly, two eggs, a glass of dry white wine, a soupspoon of Cognac, pepper, but no salt. Then add 200g of fresh cream and blend again.

Pour into a tin and sprinkle on some fresh green peppercorns and cook in a bain-marie for 10 mins on the stove and then a further 20 mins in the bain-marie in the oven covered with a sheet of tinfoil.

Cabillaud en gelée

Cod in Aspic

A jelly mould is needed for this simple and attractive starter.

Prepare a spicy court-bouillon and cook the fish ensuring that it remains firm. Leave to cool. Remove the skin and bones.

Peel some tomatoes with a sharp knife. Peel a cucumber or a courgette; cut small diamonds or other shapes into the peel. Lay the fish in the mould and decorate with the vegetables and cover with aspic. Place in the fridge for at least 3 hours. Serve with mayonnaise and a green salad.

Œufs Victoire

Boil 1 litre of milk. Set it aside. Whisk eight eggs in an ovenproof terrine and add salt and pepper. Pour in the milk with care and whisk.

Prepare a bain-marie and place the terrine in it and bake in a hot oven for 1 hour. Check the water level in the bain-marie regularly. When cooked, leave to cool a while before removing from the terrine and placing on a serving dish.
Serve with a tomato and fresh cream sauce. Decorate with parsley.

Canard façon Colombières

Colombieres-Style Duck

Cut the duck into small pieces. Brown in fat, sprinkle with flour and add 50cl of red wine and stir well. Add thyme, bay leaves, juniper berries, salt and pepper. Cook on a low heat for 45 mins.
Remove the duck and place on a dish and sieve the sauce. Put it back on the heat and add a small amount of butter with a good spoonful of cream.
Lay the duck on the plates, cover with the sauce and serve with plain rice, a chestnut purée or pears cooked in red wine.

Rôti de porc aux abricots

Roast Pork with Apricots

Brown 1.5kg roast pork with chopped shallots, sprinkle with flour and cover with stock. Add 500g of dried apricots.
Cook for 11/2 hours on a low heat in a thick-bottomed casserole dish.
Serve with sautéed potatoes, rice or spinach.

Gâteau aux marrons

Chestnut Cake

1kg of chestnuts, 100g of chocolate, 100g of butter, 100g of sugar.
Cook the chestnuts and peel and liquidise them with a little salt.
Melt the chocolate and butter and add the sugar.
Add the chestnut purée and mix well.
Pour into a charlotte mould and tamp down firmly, then turn out on to a serving dish.
Melt a little chocolate to cover the cake. Decorate with a chestnut and serve with fresh cream.

The dining room is in the outbuildings which were converted last century. There is a beautiful collection of plates from the French East India Company:.

Good wine is also appreciated at Colombières: Count Charles de Maupeou, the owner, is the son-in-law of Thierry Manoncourt, the owner of Figeac Castle, a Saint-Emilion premier cru of which we extolled the uprightness and excellence in «Cuisine in the Chateaux of Bordeaux».

BALLEROY

Semper altius

The Chateau of Balleroy is a masterpiece by a young architect who was going to become famous: Francois Mansart. It was built in 1631 for the Councillor of State Jean II de Choisy, whose father, a companion of the Marquis d'O, bought this fief in around 1600. Facing its village and surrounded by its stables, garden, cattle-sheds, press, bakery, dairy, it is more than a classical-style castle but a model of urbanism. The estate then passed to the Harcourt family before returning to a descendant of Choisy, the wife of Jacques de La Cour, called the Marquess of Balleroy. Her descendant survived the Revolution because her doctor had her rolled in nettles and declared her to be very sick! However, Balleroy was confiscated before being bought back again by the family, sold again and then bought again. Since 1970, the Forbes family has owned the castle and they have restored it and returned it to its former beauty. It is a harmonious ensemble which houses a superb, innovative, suspended staircase, collections of paintings by Grand Masters, including one by Albert de Balleroy, and quality furnishings. The cuisine offered to us, lobster and turbot, came from the Norman coast.

Top.
Before buying Balleroy, Malcolm Forbes was a Second World War hero, Senator of the United States, Editor-in-chief of Forbes magazine and the holder of several world records for hot-air balloon crossings.

Opposite.
The castle's layout is classical in style: one central dwelling house and two pavilions. The perfect scale is based on rules from the Italian Renaissance. The moat is only symbolic, because Balleroy is a residential castle, not a defensive castle. In addition to the castle, Mansart also commissioned the village built in the shape of a Latin cross, at the top of which stands the castle. But, it is necessary to be in a hot-air balloon to see it!

The recipes of Denis Leclerc from the Manoir de la Drôme

TURBOT ET POITRINE DE COCHON DE BAYEUX, CRÈME DE MORILLES ET ASPERGES VERTES

Turbot and Bayeux Pork Belly with Morel Cream Sauce and Green Asparagus

Prepare the morel mushrooms, sauté them in butter with a chopped shallot, deglaze with Madeira and cover with 50cl of cream. Reduce and season.

Cook the asparagus. Sauté the turbot fillets in salted butter and cook fine slices of the pork belly in the frying pan.

Place the turbot and asparagus on a plate, add the sauce, the morels and the pork belly.

Bayeux pork comes from a race of pig which used to be threatened with extinction, but which has now been saved. A brotherhood ensures the promotion of this meat.

HOMARD AUX HERBES DU JARDIN ET CORAIL

Lobster with Garden Herbs and Coral

Steam the lobsters for 8 mins and leave to cool.

Cut the lobsters in half, clean them and collect the coral inside the chest cavity for the vinaigrette.

Chop the chives, chervil and tarragon. Mix with a spoonful of mustard, a dash of wine vinegar and 10cl of olive oil, salt and pepper.

Put a spoonful of olive oil in a small frying pan, heat and add the coral and the contents of the chest cavity, fry over a high heat. Add two drops of Tabasco, a dash of vinegar. Add a further 10cl of olive oil and a pinch of salt.

Lay the cooled lobster halves on plates and cover with the vinaigrette and herbs.

The huge vaulted kitchen, punctuated by four pillars, is in the basement. With its large fireplace, its bread oven, utensils and ancillary rooms, it ensured the upkeep of the house's residents.

Right.
Turbot and pork, morels and green asparagus.

Below.
Lobster with herbs, with the lawns of the dried-out moat in the background.

Crème au chocolat de Mrs Forbes

Mrs Forbes' Chocolate Cream

Boil 50cl of single cream. Whisk together four egg yolks, 80g of sugar and two pinches of cinnamon. Add the cream to this mixture and cook in the same way as custard. When ready, pour immediately over 200g of grated dark chocolate and whisk briskly. Pour into glasses and place in the fridge for 2 hours before serving with *allumettes*, small puff pastry biscuits with royal icing.

Right.
Here Mrs Forbes' Chocolate Cream is accompanied by the castle's dinner set in Sèvres porcelain. Balleroy allumettes are a local speciality.

Allumettes de Balleroy

Balleroy allumettes

According to legend, allumettes came from Balleroy and it was the village's pastry chef, also a carpenter, who got the idea from wood shavings.

Roll out a piece of puff pastry to a thickness of about 3mm and cut out 8cm long rectangular bands and coat with royal icing. Cut out 3cm wide strips and place in the oven at medium temperature until they start to colour, about 10 mins.

Royal icing: mix two egg whites with 250g of icing sugar.

The dining room: The woodwork is from the 17th century. The tureen is decorated with a hot-air balloon and is a reminder of Malcom Forbes' passion for these aerostats. The large painting depicting the death of a stag is the work of Albert de Balleroy, known, above all, for his powerful animal paintings. A friend of Manet, his work was exhibited several times in Salon. The castle is home to several of his paintings.

Fontaine-Henry

The source of history

Oilliamson. Say Williamson and you will have understood the path followed by this old Scottish family who became one of the most Norman, for it is true that here, the English Channel near Bayeux with its eloquent tapestry and near the D-Day beaches is not very wide. The Williamsons served the Kings of France in the Scottish guard and made their homes here. They came from a clan in the far north of Scotland and were thwarted allies of England. The family has been known since the 14th century.

The Château de Fontaine-Henry, which is said to have the highest roofs in France, passed to the Oilliamson family in 1898 through marriage to Hermine de Cornulier, a long-standing Breton noble family. Today, entry into the castle is through the old kitchen, the three fireplaces of which are surmounted by the coats-of-arms of the successive owners: Tilly, of which there remains a cellar and chapel. Harcourt, to whom we owe the steep roof slopes. Morais, then Boutier from Château d'Assy, then Montécler, when the castle was a farm and, Marguerie, who survived the Revolution but lost the castle's archives. Carbonnel de Canisy in the 19th century, who moved the kitchen and redesigned the ponds. Cornulier and, finally, Pierre d'Olliamson who brought together the two branches of this emblematic Renaissance castle for many years divided between lordly affirmation and agricultural reality.

As for the kitchen, it has followed the passing years, moving from the south to the centre and, then, to the north. The recipes we tasted in the long gallery used as a dining room are those of Countess d'Oilliamson, born Thérèse d'Ursel.

The façade of Fontaine-Henry juxtaposes years of construction in the styles of Charles VIII, Louis XII, Francois I and Henry II, seen here from right to left.

MENU of 5 november

Chopped Chicory Salad with Roquefort and Walnuts
Cold Joint of Veal with Oilliamson Sauce
Cheese
Apple Charlotte

Apple Charlotte

RÔTI DE VEAU BRAISÉ

Braised Veal Joint

Take a boned joint of veal loin or a piece from the cushion or the chump. Find a suitably sized casserole dish. Pour in olive oil to cover the bottom of the dish. When the oil is hot, brown the veal on both sides then reduce the heat, cover and leave to cook for an hour depending on the size of the cut. When cooked, (check it using the point of a sharp knife), place on a serving dish and leave to cool.

Veal Joint with Oilliamson Sauce

SAUCE OILLIAMSON

Oilliamson Sauce

Also called Yvette Sauce, this sauce is perfect with cold meats; add as much sugar as mustard and make in the same way as an ordinary vinaigrette: a little vinegar, salt, pepper and oil. Taste.

CHARLOTTE AUX POMMES

Apple Charlotte

Stew some russet apples, sugar to taste and add some vanilla sugar. While they are stewing, cut some slices of bread into even squares. Use the number of slices needed to suit the size of the charlotte mould used. Brown the bread in a frying pan with butter and lay it in the mould. Start by covering the bottom and then the sides. Fill the interior with the stewed apples and lay the other slices of bread on the top. Place in the oven until everything has blended together. Serve hot with double cream.

Hunting button for the Cornulier team. Motto: «I am everywhere».

CHICONS

This is the name given to chicory in Belgium.
In actual fact, it is the edible part of Witloof Chicory.
They can be used in a variety of ways as winter vegetables.

FAISAN AUX CHICONS

Pheasant with Chicons

Clean the chicory, remove the small bitter cone at the root, wash well, dry and cut into small, even strips. Melt an egg-sized piece of butter in a frying pan and add the chicory. Stir and add a small spoonful of fine sugar, a dash of lemon, salt and pepper. Cover and simmer until the chicory changes colour. Set aside while you prepare the pheasant.
The pheasant will have been plucked, emptied and cleaned. Pass it over a naked flame to burn off all the down. Bard it with fine slices of bacon and brown in an oval-shaped casserole in a mixture of butter and oil. Leave to cook for 45 mins.
Remove from the casserole, cover with tinfoil and set aside.
Throw away the fat, add a glass of water and cook over a hot flame until the water has been absorbed.
Add the chicory, stir over a gentle heat and add the fresh cream. Leave to heat. In the meantime, cut the strings on the bards of bacon, carve the pheasant and lay the pieces on a dish, leaving a hole in the middle which you will fill with the chicory and cream.

SALADE DE CHICONS CISELÉS AU ROQUEFORT ET AUX NOIX

Chopped Chicons Salad with Roquefort and Walnuts

Wash one chicon for each person.
Cut into small pieces.
Prepare a traditional vinaigrette.
Add walnuts and pieces of Roquefort. Mix it all together.
Leave to marinate for 1/2 hour.

CHICONS AUX CREVETTES GRISES

Chicons with Shrimps

A chicory salad seasoned with vinaigrette. Cook the shrimps in water, roll them in coarse salt and then remove their heads.

Far from the small, closed room used in the 19th century, here, the dining room is situated in a long gallery.

Tripes à la mode de Caen

Caen-Style Tripe

The tripe will be cooked in a luted « tripière », meaning that it is sealed and cooked in a bread oven.

Take 4kg of assorted tripe (belly, reticulum, third stomach and rennet stomach which form the four parts of a cow's stomach), which you will have soaked, blanched, chilled and cut into small squares.

Place onions, leeks and carrots in the bottom of the *tripière* – some people add apples – then add the tripe, a split foot of veal as well as a split foot of beef, some garlic cloves and a large bouquet garni and cover with leeks. Season (for 1kg, 10g of salt and 2g of pepper). And, sprinkle with beef lard. Soak with 1 litre of good quality cider, a large glass of Calvados, and water so that all the meat is covered.

Cover the tripière and seal it.

Cook in a bread oven overnight.

When finished, remove the cover, remove the tripe from the gravy from which you will skim the fat. Place the tripe back in the tripière and cover with the skimmed gravy. Serve with boiled potatoes. However, there is an easier option which is to buy it from a good delicatessen! Then, all you need to do is reheat it to enjoy it.

Grace watches over the dining room. This is a copy by Aubry, an 18th century Norman painter, of a famous painting by Chardin.

Andouille à la Bovary

Bovary-Style Chitterlings Sausage

Prepare some small savoury pancakes of the same size as a slice of chitterlings sausage with a 1cm edge. Cook some spinach and sorrel, place on a serving dish, add a small hot pancake and place a slice of chitterlings sausage on the top, which, when it comes into contact with the heat of the pancake, will reach the desired temperature.

Sablés de Caen

Caen-Style Shortbread Biscuits

250g of flour, 125g of sugar, a flavouring of your choice, 250g of butter and the crushed and sieved yolks of three boiled eggs, a pinch of salt. Leave the dough for an hour. Roll out to a thickness of 5cm and use a fluted cutter to cut out biscuits measuring about 4cm in diameter.
Lay on a lightly moistened tray and criss-cross with the point of a knife. Place in a hot oven for 6 to 8 mins.

The cutlery bears the Cornulier coat-of-arms - Le Doulcet de Méré.

Bourdots

Also called « douillons », these desserts are typically Norman. They are made either with apples or pears.

Prepare a shortcrust pastry with 250g of flour, 125g of softened butter, a pinch of salt and a little water. Form a ball of pastry mixture and leave for 1 hour.
Prepare four apples: peel them, but keep the stalk. Sprinkle a little caster or brown sugar over them and add a knob of butter or honey. You may also add a little cinnamon or another spice according to taste.
Take your pastry mixture and cut it into four squares. Place the apples on them with care and fold the pastry over them, leaving the stalk of the apple sticking out if necessary. Wet your fingers to seal the pastry.
Whisk an egg yolk with a little water. Glaze the *bourdots* and cut out a decoration with the point of a knife. Cook in a hot oven for about 30 mins.

Fontaine-Etoupefour

Re-naissance

Many castles in Normandy disappeared during times of war. Without the unfailing devotion of Count and Countess Henri du Laz, Fontaine-Etoupefour would be no more than a memory. A souvenir of hill 112, the position held by the Germans one month after the D-Day Landings of 6 June 1944, bombarded by the Allies and retaken by the Germans. On the day of the liberation of Caen, on 10 July, 45,000 shells fell around the castle and the Germans abandoned their injured soldiers in the castle's cellars. Later, when the moats were cleaned, 400 shells, objects fallen from the castle and souvenirs from former times were found.

This war put an end to the confrontations inflicted on an old seigniory owned by the same family since 1538. The name of Fontaine-Etoupefour, which is also the name of the village, is probably a reminder of the existence of tow ovens: we know that there was a fulling mill on the castle's land, next to the gardens and the orchards which have now disappeared. The succession of owners is simple: the castle dates from 1583 and was owned by Le Valois family. Then, through marriage, it passed to the Barons of Blangy and through inheritance to Count Henri du Laz. The war completed the ruin of the castle, which had already lost its roof in a fire. The postern has been converted into a dwelling house, which is small but pleasant, with a unique dining room below the former porch. No doubt, one day, the Renaissance jewel of Château de Fontaine-Etoupefour will be rebuilt.

Today, Fontaine-Etoupefour's postern is a dwelling house. A tall building - accentuated by a series of cylindrical and octagonal towers and conical pinnacle turrets - it dates from the end of the 15th century. Nothing could be more elegant than this narrow building situated at the side of the wide moat.

Menu of 13 january

Fish Terrine with Lamb's Lettuce
Chicken with Camembert
Cheese
English Shortbread with Custard

Alsace Wine
Bordeaux Wine
Vallois Champagne in memory of the founding family

Poulet au camembert

Chicken with Camembert

This is a recipe from nearby Château de Juvigny, another of the family's properties, where Henry du Laz grew up. The Chef was called Céline Leroty; a name which favoured good food. She also used to make excellent chocolate profiteroles.

Choose a good farm chicken and a very good Camembert, such as the ones made in Normandy.

Preheat the oven. Remove the Camembert's crust and cut it into small pieces and place them inside the chicken with a little tarragon, salt and pepper. Close the chicken with a little cooking thread. Sprinkle a little curry powder over the skin of the chicken and place it in a dish with half a glass of water at the bottom. Cook in the oven for about 45 mins. Check it with a sharp knife. If the tip of the knife is boiling hot, the chicken is cooked.

Brown some salsify in butter with some finely sliced mushrooms. Add garlic, salt and pepper. Remove the chicken from the oven and leave to cool before carving. Cooking will have produced a creamy sauce with the Camembert having melted and leaked slowly out of the chicken. Carve the chicken and serve the sauce separately. Serve the vegetables on the plate with the chicken. Enjoy your meal.

We loved this dish, as did Camille and Alice, the granddaughters of Monsieur and Madame du Laz... that is until they were told what was in it!

Left page.
An old hot chocolate pot and stirring stick. The lid has a hole for inserting the small stick.

Bottom right.
English Shortbread.

Lapin à la moutarde

Rabbit with mustard

For a 1kg rabbit cut into pieces, whisk about 180g of fromage frais gradually adding three soup-spoons of corn flour and the desired amount of strong mustard, depending on whether you like mustard or not. Coat the rabbit pieces with this mixture. Lay them out on a sheet of tinfoil at the bottom of an oven dish, sprinkle with thyme, salt and pepper. Cover with another sheet of tinfoil. Cook in a hot oven for 50 to 60 mins.

Galette anglaise

English Shortbread

Recipe from Madame Eloffe's family, Madame du Laz's mother. « This shortbread biscuit is similar to Breton shortbread biscuits but is thicker ».

Mix 125g of sugar with an egg and 125g of softened butter, then add 250g of flour. Mix with a fork to form a very soft paste.

Place in a buttered and floured baking tin and pat down firmly with a glass, the bottom of which has been dipped in flour.

Criss-cross with a knife dipped in flour or else the dough will tear. Place in a hot oven for a quarter of an hour and cut it when hot or warm.

Store in a metal or plastic box.

Serve with custard: boil 50cl of milk with half a vanilla pod. In a bowl, whisk four egg yolks and 80g of sugar. Remove the vanilla pods and pour the hot milk on to the mixture stirring constantly with a wooden spoon. Place back on the heat to thicken, but do not let it boil. Serve in a sauce boat (here in Paris porcelain).

Pain de thon de madame Eloffe

Madame Eloffe's Tuna Bread

One of Madame du Laz's pleasurable childhood memories.

Grind the contents of a large tin of tuna. Make a very thick white sauce and mix everything together with a beaten egg, salt and pepper. Pour into a ring-shaped mould and cook gently in a bain-marie and use a sharp knife to check whether it is cooked. Prepare a tomato purée.
Remove the bread from the mould and serve with the tomato purée poured into the centre.

Charlotte aux amandes

Charlotte with Almonds

100g of softened butter, 100g of sugar, 100g of powdered almonds, 100g of fresh cream. Mix these ingredients together. Cover the bottom of a charlotte mould with sponge biscuits which have been coated with a thick syrup. Fill with successive layers of almond cream and sponge biscuits and finish with a layer of sponge biscuits. Place in the fridge.

Count and Countess Henry du Laz in their extraordinary dining room installed in the postern's porch.

Top.
« La montagne de Vilard marchand en sa maison a Vilard et Jean? Qui luy donné de la poterie de Balleroy », are the words on this Balleroy Calvados jug. As with hundreds of other very old bottles, it was found in the castle's moat.

Right page.
Fontaine-Etoupefour, still intact in the 19th century.

Malakoff

This dessert was given by the family of Madame du Laz's sister. It is best if two people make it.

Stiffen six egg whites until a spoon is able to stay upright in the mixture, then add a heaped soup-spoon of sugar for each egg white and fold into the mixture. Make a caramel sauce with six heaped spoonfuls of sugar and a very small amount of water because the caramel must be hard. This is where there needs to be two of you because you have to be fast and good with your hands: pour in the boiling caramel while stirring vigorously; one stirs while the other holds the bowl. Pour the mixture into a smooth-sided and oiled mould and place somewhere cool, but not too cold. The next day, remove it from its mould, serve with custard and watch it float.

CANON

Walls and whispers

« I thought that you fully owned Canon but I see that, making a play on words, you need a canon to enter your home… » In this letter, Voltaire ironised the never-ending trial which, finally, allowed Jean-Baptiste Elie de Beaumont to retake possession of the fief of Canon, sold in 1727 by an ancestor of his wife over a background of religious dispute: the Berenger family whose forefathers were Protestants. Elie de Beaumont was a famous lawyer. Once the trial was won, he added a storey to the castle and Italian-style balusters and created a park which has since become famous. The farm was organised according to the principles of the «*Encyclopaedia*». Everything appears to be well-ordered, yet, the frontons bear the maxims of Boileau where the spirit of Light blows and evocations of the *Fête des Bonnes Gens*. Also, at first sight, the park appears to be very classical with its needle-straight perspectives, but loses its way and twists and turns into more English-style fantasies. Exotic creations, neo-classical ruins, astonishing mottos on the frontons, water games, waterfalls, many surprises before discovering the faultless layout of the Chartreuses, gardens enclosed behind high walls, home to vegetables from many different horizons. The teachings of the *Encyclopaedia* are full of surprises!

«Canon is a cancer which is eating me», wrote Elie de Beaumont, hugely in debt from all the works. His descendents took over the task of maintaining a property which suffered a great deal during the Second World War and successive storms. Through succession, today, Canon belongs to the Mézerac family.

Top.
«Two pigeons love each other tenderly». The motto on a Renaissance dovecote cut in two to make place for an alley.
Opposite.
This Chinese kiosk at the end of a shady alley comes from Château des Ternes in Paris. It is one of the «creations» in the Canon park.

The old recipe books of the Elie de Beaumont family

MATELOTE DE SOLES FAÇON CAEN

Caen-Style Sole Matelote

This type of recipe is common in the old recipe books found in the drawers of old furniture. There are no measurements, no logic in the recipe's progression, but, at the end, an appeal to the dexterity and foresight of the Chef who only made a note of what was essential.

«Place the fish on a dish with a few pieces of butter around it, salt, pepper, a little warm water, fines herbes and a little white wine; for the fines herbes: whites of chives and very little parsley. At the end, add fresh butter to bind the sauce and always stir in the same direction tilting the dish so that the sauce is all on the same side. At the same time as the fish, add the mussels and mushrooms. When the sauce has the same consistency as cream, sprinkle the fish with breadcrumbs and serve in the dish which was used to cook it.»

The castle's rear façade overlooks a long body of water and a park scattered with creations and statues.

Petites galettes d'Arromanches

Small Arromanches Shortbread Biscuits

Take a pound of flour, 250g of sugar, 250g of butter, knead together to form a dough, wet your fingers or add a drop of water if the dough is too sticky.

Roll it out to the same thickness as a 5 Franc coin; cut out the biscuits with a Bordeaux wine glass. Butter a baking tin and cook in the oven at a low heat. They are even better when four egg yolks are added. Glaze with a little egg yolk before putting them in the oven. Keep these biscuits in tin boxes. Quantities for about sixty biscuits. »

Written inventory of the property of Elie de Beaumont.

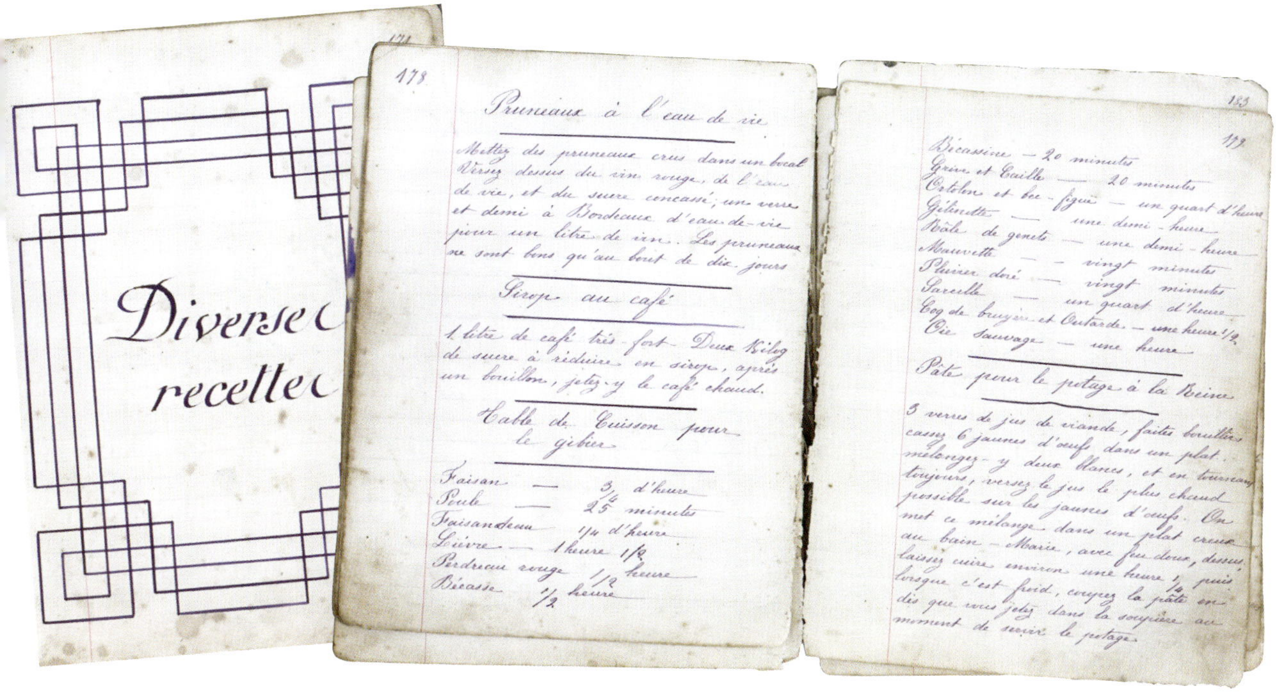

Diverses recettes

178

Pruneaux à l'eau de vie

Mettez des pruneaux crus dans un bocal. Versez dessus du vin rouge, de l'eau de vie, et du sucre concassé; un verre et demi à Bordeaux d'eau-de-vie pour un litre de vin. Les pruneaux ne sont bons qu'au bout de dix jours

Sirop au café

1 litre de café très fort. Deux kilog de sucre à réduire en sirop, après un bouillon, jetez-y le café chaud.

Table de Cuisson pour le gibier

Faisan — 3/4 d'heure
Poule — 25 minutes
Faisandeau 1/4 d'heure
Lièvre — 1 heure 1/2
Perdreau rouge 1/2 heure
Bécasse 1/2 heure

179

Bécassine — 20 minutes
Grive et Caille — 20 minutes
Ortolan et bec-figue — un quart d'heure
Gélinotte — une demi-heure
Râle de genets — une demi-heure
Mauvette — vingt minutes
Pluvier doré — vingt minutes
Sarcelle — un quart d'heure
Coq de bruyère et Outarde — une heure 1/2
Oie sauvage — une heure

Pâte pour le potage à la Reine

3 verres de jus de viande, faites bouillir, cassez 6 jaunes d'oeufs dans un plat, mélangez-y deux blancs, et en tournant toujours, versez le jus le plus chaud possible sur les jaunes d'oeufs. On met ce mélange dans un plat creux au bain-Marie, avec feu doux, dessus, laissez cuire environ une heure 1/4, puis lorsque c'est froid, coupez la pâte en dés que vous jetez dans la soupière au moment de servir le potage.

Canon is also the head office of a farm which has an enormous ancient press. It produces Cider, Calvados, Poiré, Pommeau and Halbi, which is a retake of a very old recipe. They can be found in Hervé de Mézerac's cellar, near an astonishing farm occupied by Peruvian llamas and Hungarian woolly pigs. In the 20th century, still, a « white farm » bred chickens, rabbits, turkeys, ducks and other animals... all white, even the cat.

Aspic
de pommes

Apple Aspic

Peel 1kg of apples combining different varieties (Rambaud and Belles de Boskop for example). Cook gently with 750g of sugar per kilo until they turn red and caramelised. Pour into bowls to give the mixture a form which you will turn out on to a dish just before serving, and serve with vanilla cream for example.

We photographed this confit apple-coloured dessert in the Chartreuses of Canon, in front of Rose Campion and Spiderwort.

This register lists all the practices for the Fête des Bonnes Gens instituted in 1775: resolutions, recommendations, celebrations, etc. for this festivity rewarding virtuous girls, good fathers and mothers and kindly elderly people according to carefully defined criteria: a « good old person » should, in particular, have planted many apple and pear trees and have won agricultural prizes.

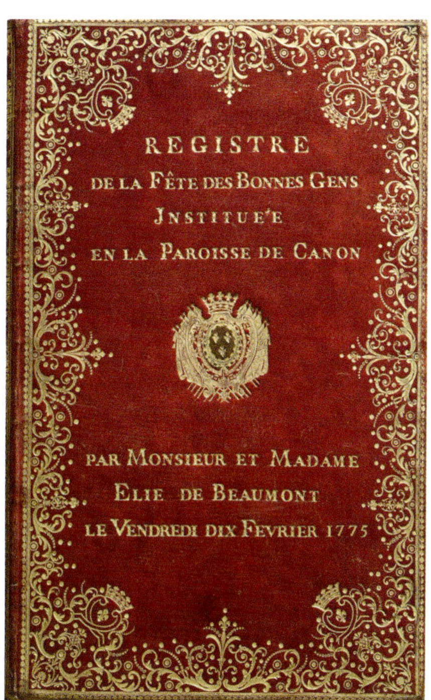

Bon jeune homme

175g of dark chocolate broken into pieces,
125g of caster sugar,
3 glasses of milk.

Mix together the chocolate, sugar and milk in a thick-bottomed pan and cook over a low heat. Stir often and leave for 45 mins until you have obtained a thick paste. Pour the cream into small pots and leave to cool. It is possible to prepare these pots in advance and keep in the fridge. They may also be served with a vanilla cream.

The recipe for «Bon Jeune Homme» in the park of Canon. What is the reason behind this intriguing name? Once again, it is a family tradition. When the family received a future son-in-law, the meal ended with these words: «Now we are going to taste this nice young man! » (bon jeune homme)*. This ritual is very similar to one we encountered at Château de Rully in Burgundy. The* bons jeunes hommes *in their china pots match the beautiful statues of Canon-les-Bonnes-Gens.*

The thirteen gardens enclosed by high walls known as the Chartreuses are a conservatory for plants from all over the world, as well as an invitation to meditation, created by Elie de Beaumont in order to rest and « not even open a book ». The height of the southern walls have turned it into an open-air greenhouse.

Vénitienne au kirsch

Venitienne with Kirsch

125g of butter,
125g of caster sugar.
1 teacup of milk,
4 soup-spoons of kirsch.

Soften the butter in front of the oven. Place it in a terrine and add the sugar and cream together until the paste has whitened. Add the warm milk drop by drop stirring constantly as if for a mayonnaise. When the paste is smooth, add the kirsch stirring constantly. Pour the paste into a mould filled with sponge biscuits dipped in kirsch and then place in the fridge. It is best to prepare it the day before serving.

Conservation du jus de fraises

Conserving Strawberry Juice

« Conserving strawberry juice is the same as conserving tomatoes. Crush the strawberries (small ones preferably) and strain through a linen cloth. Pour the juice into bottles. Place the bottles in a boiler filled with cold water and surround the bottles with hay. Boil for 1/2 hour and leave to cool in the water. Then store the bottles somewhere cool. »

Vendeuvre

Surprises and miniatures

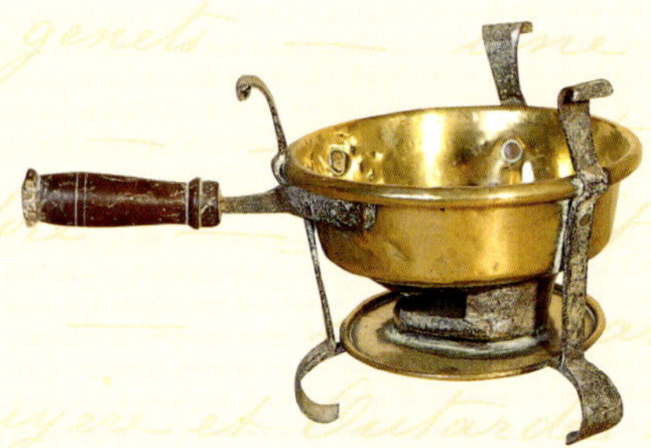

The Chateau de Vendeuvre in the commune of Vendeuvre, belongs to the Count and Countess of Vendeuvre. But, it is not as simple as that, because it is a castle full of surprises. In this beautiful «rural home», built in record time between 1750 and 1752, there are many astonishing collections and creations. The Second World War saw the castle occupied, emptied, damaged, dug up and bombarded. Today it is restored and illustrates the fruit of Guy and Elyane de Vendeuvre's passions: for him (largely) the excavation of a large pond on the southern façade; the water gardens and the park's follies; the seashell cave; and the maze and various gardens. For her (mainly) the collection, dating from the tender age of seven, of all types of miniatures, tiny niches, dolls' kitchens; carefully assembled masterpieces by master tradesmen; more than seven hundred items, the first museum in the world of miniature furniture, and some new surprises…

Both of them also love good food, old cooking utensils and good recipes, some of which are presented here. Some come from the notebooks of Aunt Germaine, a great-aunt of Monsieur de Vendeuvre, who died at the age of 103 years. Others come from the family of Elyane de Vendeuvre, born de Grimouärd. And, to all, the Vendeuvre motto: «Neither regret for the past nor fear of the future.»

Top.
The portable stove on which the «tripière» is placed for reheating Caen-style tripe.
Opposite.
Everything can be found in the old kitchen of Vendeuvre: the rare Pre d'Auge (in the foreground), a crayfish buisson, *an old coffee mill… as well as a fireplace (for roasting), a* potager *(for stewing), an oven (for the bread).*

Apéritif Cinzano

Cinzano Aperitif

1l of red wine,
200g of granulated sugar,
20 camomile flowers,
40g of orange peel,
a glass of eau-de-vie.

Leave to macerate for fifteen days. Then filter.

Sandwich Claude

Make a mustard mayonnaise, liquidise two boiled eggs and a large bunch of mint and mix it all together. Spread on bread of your choice.

Where does this small terrine with its unusual fleur-de-lys come from? And what about the large hare-shaped one? Mystery and miniatures...

Pâté de lapin

Rabbit Paté

Take a wild rabbit, cut into pieces as for a rabbit stew, but do not remove the bones (only use the hind, or, at least, remove the head). If you use a domestic rabbit, marinate it for two or three days beforehand and, drain it well before serving. Place a large, very fine strip of bacon at the bottom of a large mould, then add a layer of rabbit, well compacted but not overlapping, and salt and pepper and spices if you wish. Then add another layer of very fine bacon strips, a layer of rabbit, salt, etc. Continue until all the rabbit has been used. Finish with a layer of bacon and cook in a bain-marie for at least 5 or 6 hours – taking care to add water to the bain-marie and ensuring that it boils constantly. Leave to cool and only remove from the mould in order to serve the next day or the day after.

Lièvre à la royale

Hare à la Royale

Place the hare in an iron cocotte dish after tying it. Brown it at a low heat. Prepare a mincemeat with the liver, 500g of bacon, shallots and parsley. Boil a full bowl of garlic, drain and add to the stuffing. This will serve as a thickener for the stuffing. Add a glass or 1/2 glass of vinegar (depending on its strength) and two glasses of red wine.

Mix together and pour over the hare in the cocotte dish whilst hot. Add the blood from the hare and stir with a little wine. Add eight to ten sugar cubes. Leave to cook at a low heat for 5 to 6 hours. Serve with small fried croutons.

Fricandeau sauce Vendeuvre

Fricandeau with Vendeuvre Sauce

Cook a fricandeau (thick slice of cushion of veal) in its juices, or a good piece of thick round of veal. When it is cooked and about 20 to 25 mins before serving, remove from the pan but keep warm. Take an egg-sized piece of very fresh butter, mix into the flour and place it into the sauce left from the fricandeau, with a large half-glass of cream. Leave to cook and stir from time to time.

This preparation should be cooked for 15 to 20 mins and must be brought to the boil so that the flour thickens and turns a golden or russet colour. The next day it is excellent when served cold, the ideal hot-cold sauce.

The dining room at Vendeuvre faces west. The Caen damask tablecloth depicts the castle lit by the last rays of sunlight. The highchair is a dream for gourmet babies and used to belong to Louis-Ferdinande de Vendeuvre.

Brochet Sancerre à la crème

Pike with Sancerre Cream

Cook the pike on a bed of carrots and onions, cover with Sancerre white wine and add butter, salt and pepper. Cover with tinfoil and use a knife to check whether it is cooked.
The sauce: prepare a roux and soak with the cooking juices.
Before serving: add an egg yolk, fresh cream and lemon juice (for 50cl of sauce, use two spoonfuls of cream, one egg yolk and the juice of one lemon).

Rognons belle gourmande

Kidneys Belle Gourmande

In a high-sided frying pan, brown some chipolata sausages in butter and when they are golden brown remove them and add the trimmed kidneys.
Chop some shallots and mushrooms and add them to the kidneys. When they are very hot, add some tarragon. Leave to cook. Deglaze with port. Add the chipolatas and finish cooking. Serve with mashed potatoes and decorate with tarragon leaves.

Coffee grill, toaster… old-style cooking was very clever.

At the age of 7 years, Elyane de Vendeuvre was spellbound by a small marquetry escritoire at the house of an elderly aunt. She bequeathed it to her on her death and it formed the start of her collection. After years of research, today, Vendeuvre presents an amazing collection of small masterpieces such as this miniature kitchen which contains about ten items.

Pommes de terre

Potatoes

Something amusing to do with children

Crush 500g of madeleine sponge cakes or biscuits with a large piece of butter to form a soft paste.

Add a few spoonfuls of rum, add some grated and melted chocolate and a few oven-grilled almonds. Roll into potato shapes and prick holes for the eyes.

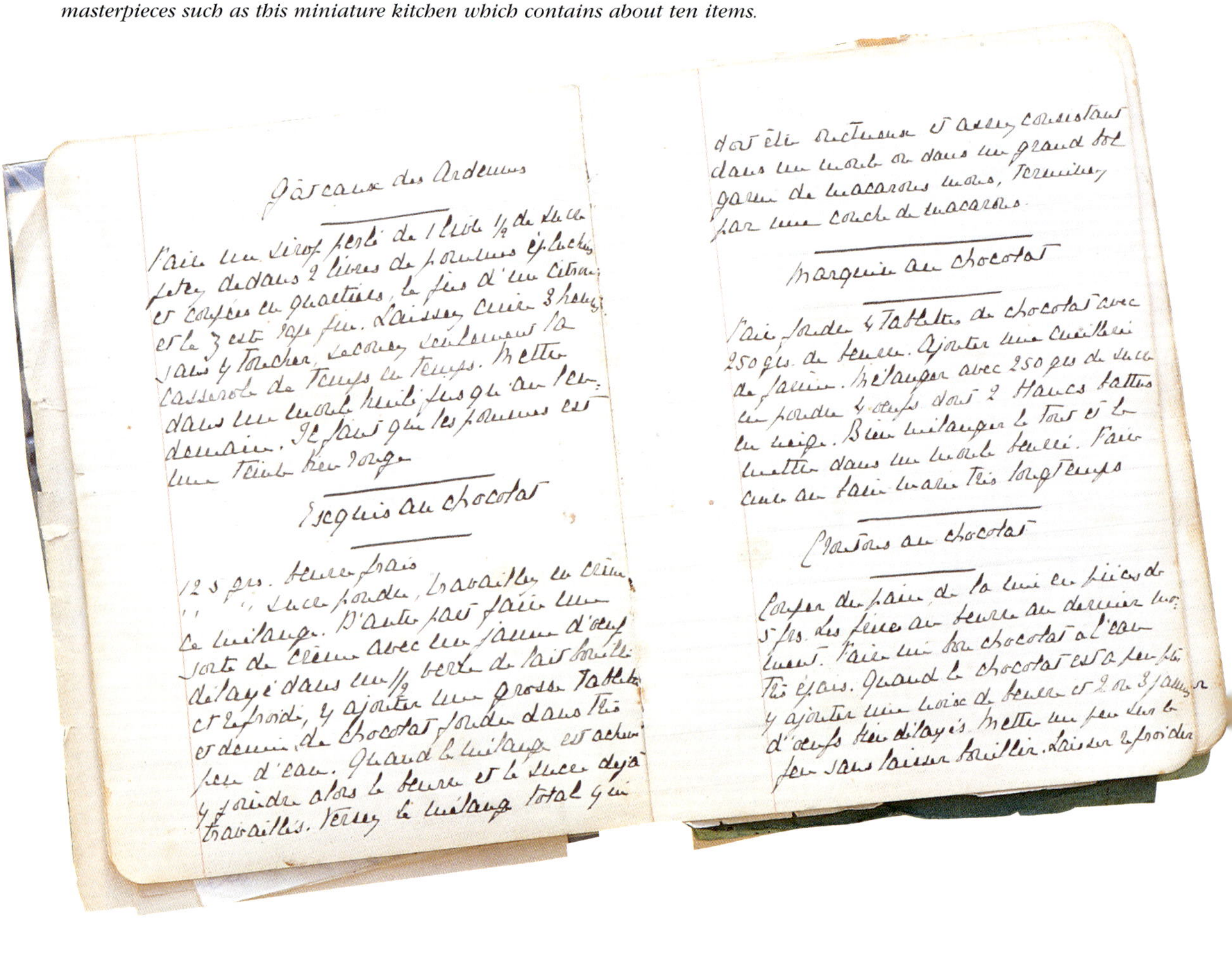

Gâteau des Ardennes

Faire un sirop perlé de 1 livre 1/2 de sucre, jetez dedans 2 livres de pommes épluchées et coupées en quartiers, le jus d'un citron et le zeste sapé fin. Laissez cuire 3 heures sans y toucher, secouez seulement la casserole de temps en temps. Mettez dans un moule huilé jusqu'au lendemain. Il faut que les pommes est une teinte bien rouge.

Exquis au chocolat

125 grs. beurre frais
" " sucre poudre, travaillez en crème le mélange. D'autre part faire une sorte de crème avec un jaune d'œuf délayé dans un 1/2 verre de lait bouilli et refroidi, y ajouter une grosse tablette et demie de chocolat fondu dans très peu d'eau. Quand le mélange est achevé y joindre alors le beurre et le sucre déjà travaillés. Versez le mélange total qui doit être onctueux et assez consistant dans un moule ou dans un grand bol garni de macarons mous, terminez par une couche de macarons.

Marquise au chocolat

Faire fondre 4 tablettes de chocolat avec 250 grs. de beurre. Ajouter une cuillerée de farine. Mélanger avec 250 grs de sucre en poudre 4 œufs dont 2 blancs battus en neige. Bien mélanger le tout et le mettre dans un moule beurré. Faire cuire au bain marie très longtemps

Croûtons au chocolat

Couper du pain de la veille en pièces de 5 cm. les frire au beurre au dernier moment. Faire un bon chocolat à l'eau très épais. Quand le chocolat est à peu près y ajouter une noix de beurre et 2 ou 3 jaunes d'œufs bien délayés. Mettez un peu sur le feu sans laisser bouillir. Laisser refroidir

DIABLOTINS À LA NORMANDE

Normandy-Style Diablotins

Melt 40g of butter and mix with a large spoonful of flour and rice cream. Add a cupful of milk, salt and pepper and bring to the boil stirring all the time. The mixture should be thick. Add 60g of Camembert with the crust removed and cut into cubes. When the cheese has melted, spread the mixture at a thickness of about 2cm on a buttered and floured oven tray. Leave to cool and cut into pieces. Coat them twice by dipping them in egg and then in breadcrumbs and fry them at the last minute in very hot fat. Add some cayenne pepper to the mixture.

ROYAL AU CHOCOLAT

Chocolate Royal

Melt 150g of butter, add three tablets of chocolate and once it has all melted remove from the heat and whisk in four spoonfuls of granulated sugar, three egg yolks and the stiffened egg whites. Cook in a bain-marie for half an hour. Remove from the mould once it has cooled. Serve with whipped cream or custard.

Vendeuvre: a beautiful 18th century country house which became a 20th century folly.

Royal aux pommes

Apple Royal

Take 500g of stewed Russet apples. Add 500g of vanilla sugar. Melt four sheets of gelatine in a cup of water and mix with the cold stewed apples. Whisk the mixture firmly until it starts to foam. Pour into a lightly oiled mould and leave to set until the following day. Turn out the royal and serve with a rum or kirsch cream.

Diplomate normand au calvados

Norman Diplomate with Calvados

Every year, Madame de Vendeuvre gives her visitors one of the house's old recipes. Here is one of them.

Cook 1kg of peeled and finely sliced apples for half an hour with two pieces of fresh butter until you have obtained compote. Take a glass of Calvados mixed with a glass of water and soak sponge biscuits in it and line the bottom of a charlotte mould with them. Add a layer of apple compote. Cover with a layer of soaked sponge biscuits then a layer of raspberry jelly. Soak 100g of Malaga grapes in a glass of water. Add to the charlotte and then continue with the successive layers following the same order as at the beginning until you reach the top of the mould. Finish with a layer of soaked sponge biscuits.

Leave to cool for one night with a weight on top in order to settle it. Remove from the mould and decorate with candied fruit. Serve with vanilla cream.

Norman Diplomate with Calvados.

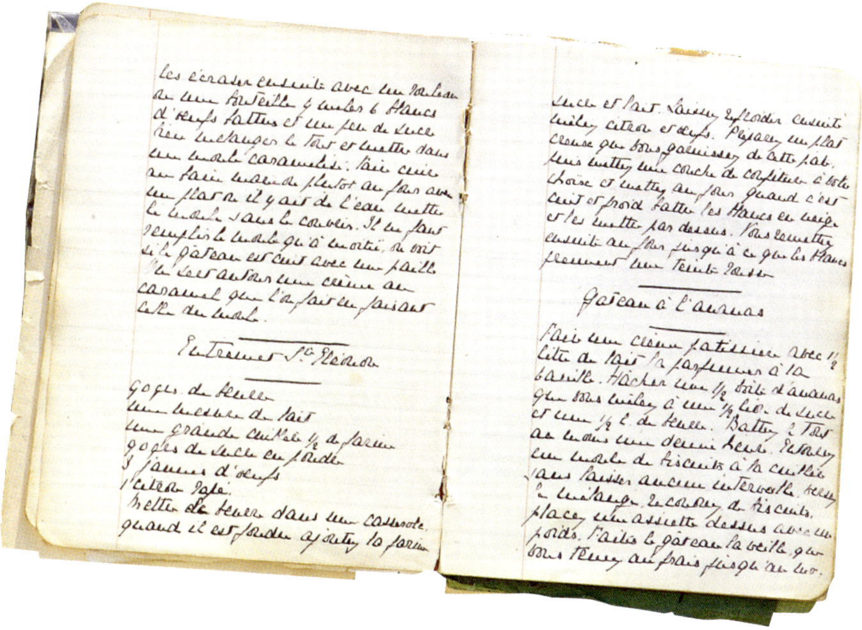

les écraser ensuite avec un rouleau
ou une bouteille y mêler 6 blancs
d'œufs battus et un peu de sucre
bien mélanger le tout et mettre dans
un moule caramélisé. Faire cuire
au bain marie ou plutôt au four avec
un plat où il y ait de l'eau mettre
le moule dans le couvercle. Il ne faut
remplir le moule qu'à moitié, on voit
si le gâteau est cuit avec une paille
on sert autour une crème au
caramel que l'on fait en faisant
celui du moule.

Entremets Ste Eléonore

90 gr de beurre
une mesure de lait
une grande cuillère 1/2 de farine
90 gr de sucre en poudre
3 jaunes d'œufs
1 citron râpé.
Mettre le beurre dans une casserole.
quand il est fondu ajoutez la farine

sucre et lait. Laissez refroidir ensuite
mêlez citron et œufs. Préparez un plat
creux que vous garnissez de cette pâte.
Puis mettez une couche de confiture à votre
choix et mettez au four quand c'est
cuit et froid battre les blancs en neige
et les mettre par dessus. Vous remettez
ensuite au four jusqu'à ce que les blancs
prennent une teinte rosée

Gâteau à l'ananas

Faire une crème pâtissière avec 1/2
litre de lait la parfumer à la
vanille. Hacher une 1/2 boîte d'ananas
que vous mêlez à une 1/2 livre de sucre
et une 1/2 l. de beurre. Battez le tout
au moins une demi heure. Garnissez
un moule de biscuits à la cuillère
sans laisser aucun intervalle, versez
le mélange, recouvrez de biscuits,
placez une assiette dessus avec un
poids. Faites le gâteau la veille, que
vous tenez au frais jusqu'au lendemain.

Petits fours glacés

Glazed Petits Fours

Walnuts, prunes and dates.

Preparing the marzipan: three-quarters of a bowl of granulated sugar, 100g of crushed biscuits, 100g of almond powder, 100g of melted butter and a dash of milk.

Form three balls (natural colour for the prunes, green for the walnuts and pink for the dates).

Decorate the fruit with the marzipan the day before glazing.

Preparing the glazing syrup: 400g of granulated sugar mixed with three-quarters of a glass of water and a soup-spoon of vinegar. Heat over a hot flame taking care to wet the sides of the pan with a damp cloth (use a small stick). Leave to cook and check the syrup by dipping your cloth on the stick in it. The syrup is ready when it is transparent and hardens in the water.

Glazing: place the glaze over a very low heat and with a spoon, dip the petits fours into the syrup one by one. Stir quickly and lay them on a lightly oiled tray. When they have cooled, remove them, use a knife to cut any excess glazing and serve them in tiny dishes or paper cake cups. The quantities given are for 50 petits fours.

These petits fours were served to us on one of the castle's miniature dinner sets.

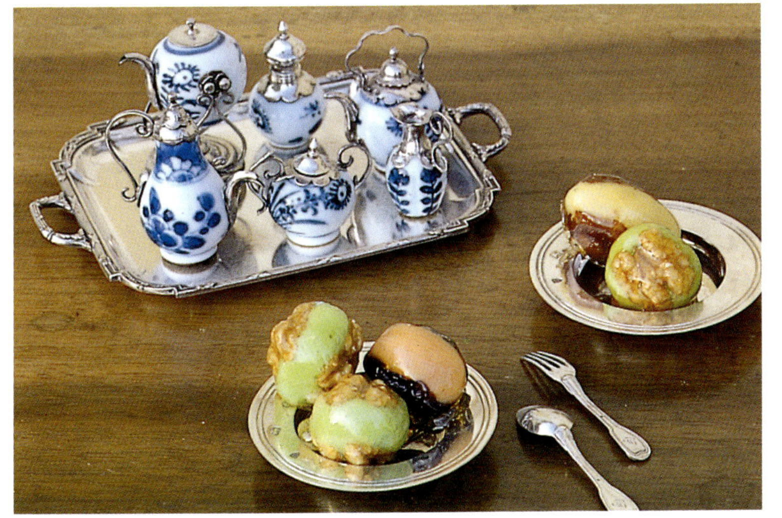

Couronne de pommes en biscuit au calvados

Sponge Biscuit Apple Crown with Calvados

Another recipe given to visitors by Madame de Vendeuvre

Break three eggs into a clean earthenware bowl, add two measures (two cups) of ground sugar, add 100g of melted, unsalted butter and 100g of freshly curdled milk (or a yoghurt), and two measures of sieved flour.

Beat these ingredients together firmly and sprinkle on some powdered vanilla (a sachet of vanilla sugar) and a pinch of yeast (a half sachet of baking powder); peel and slice three apples and a pear and add them to the mixture. Mix carefully adding two glasses of Calvados. Pour into a copper jelly mould greased with butter. Cook for 45 mins in a hot oven.

LE CHAMP-VERSANT

A manor in Auge

Without a doubt, this is the most emblematic image of Normandy: a small timber-framed manor, with buildings scattered haphazardly around the fields and orchards. The Pays d'Auge, which straddles Calvados and Eure, has preserved its freshness. The Manoir du Champ-Versant takes its name from its location on a plateau which divides the Dive and Touque basins. Its foundations are in sandstone and flint to prevent the upwelling of damp and to support the oak framework. The door is surmounted by a gracious brace bearing the coat-of-arms. The house is pegged, light but sturdy. Two small towers at the rear give it a seigniorial aspect. The construction dates from 1560, no doubt on top of an ancient stronghold with moats which have since been filled. Monsieur Letrésor's family bought it in 1893 and since then they have assured its upkeep. Thirty years ago, the decision was taken to demolish the manor's ten Napoleon III fireplaces. Behind them, ten 18th century fireplaces were found and behind them ten monumental stone fireplaces which can be seen today. They have restored to Champ-Versant its atmosphere of former times.

Madame Letrésor's cuisine is that of her generous region. Her grandmother's notebooks charmed us with their quality and freshness.

The pond is an essential part of the manor in the Pays d'Auge.
This one has kept its wash-house with its floating floor regulated by two trammels.

The recipes from the notebook of Madame Letrésor's grandmother

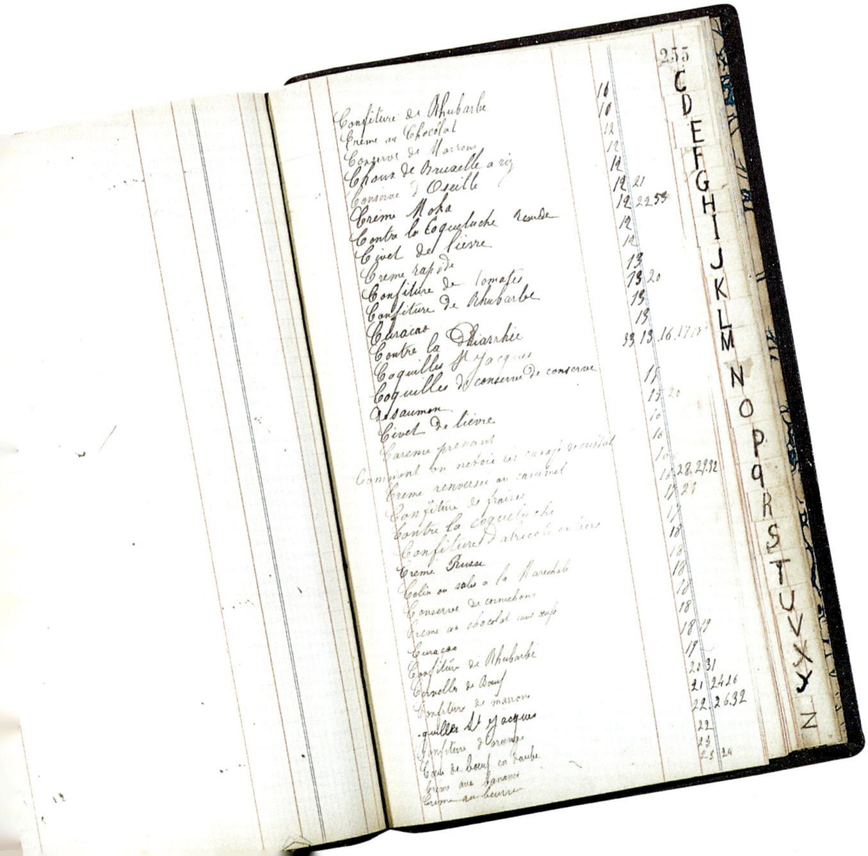

An old collection of writings combining cookery and body care.

A marvellous remedy for nails and abscesses

A large spoonful of olive oil, a large spoonful of dark honey from Brittany, an egg yolk.

Mix with a wooden spoon gradually adding buckwheat flour until a creamy consistency is obtained and apply to the abscess. Repeat two or three times a day.

Remedy for burns

Three spoonfuls of olive oil and one egg. Mix together well and add twelve drops of laudanum and twenty-four drops of alkali. Mix all the ingredients together. Place this unguent in a hermetically sealed container; apply it with a feather to silk paper which will then be applied to the burn. Apply the unguent several times a day to the outside of the paper without removing it. The paper will fall off once the burn has healed completely.

Top.
Le Médecin dans la Poche.
« In the centre of the handkerchief, a reproduction of a scene evoking the work of a travelling doctor at a fair. Around the edges of the handkerchief, 24 vignettes in which the methods for treating various ills are shown: burns, sprains and strains, whitlows and indigestion, etc. The original document was engraved by Buquet in around 1875 in Rouen. »

Chicken with White Wine.

Bouchées aux crevettes

Prawn Vol-au-Vents

Peel a quart of mixed shrimps and prawns. In a saucepan, melt 25g of butter and stir in a heaped spoonful of flour. Add a small amount of stock and bind with an egg yolk. Add the prawns and shrimps and fill the vol-au-vent cases which can be bought from bakers.
Note: heat in a very hot oven for 5 mins before serving.

Sole normande

Normandy Sole

Here is an original Normandy Sole: without cream!

This dish can be made only with average-sized fillets of sole or whole soles. After preparing the fish, place it in a buttered ovenproof dish and soak with half of white wine and half the cooking juices of mushrooms. Bake at a low heat after covering it with a piece of buttered greaseproof paper. Once it is cooked, lay the sole on the serving dish and surround it with cooked mussels, blanched oysters and cooked mushrooms and keep warm. Reduce three quarts of the sole's juices and add a light roux. Remove from the heat, butter the sauce and add a little Cayenne pepper. Pour the sauce over the sole. Decorate the dish with some crayfish cooked in a court-bouillon and some small toasted and buttered croutons.

Poule au blanc

Chicken with White Wine

A 1.5kg Crèvecoeur chicken, salt, pepper, three cloves, two onions, six carrots, three leeks, a stick of celery, a bouquet garni, fresh cream, salsify.
Place the chicken in a cooking pot, cover it with cold water and bring to the boil slowly. Add salt and, around the chicken, add various vegetables and the bouquet garni. Bring back to the boil and leave to stew for 1 1/2 hours.
Remove 1l of stock to cook the salsify separately and fry a few mushrooms in butter. Carve the chicken and lay the pieces on a hot serving dish. Lay the well-drained vegetables around it.
Heat the cream and add the mushrooms which have been fried in butter. Serve the cream in a sauceboat after pouring a few spoonfuls over the pieces of chicken.

Ile d'amour

Whisk eight egg whites until stiff; add 15g of caster sugar and candied fruit: orange peel, lemon peel, citron peel, sliced angelica, whole cherries, apricot paste, cubed raspberries.
Pour everything into a mould coated with caramel, pressing down well, and cook in a bain-marie for about 1 1/2 hours. Remove from the mould and serve with a good vanilla cream which is not too thick. The very light cake should float on the surface.

Terrine à la paysanne

Farm-Style Terrine

This dish is very cheap and greatly appreciated.

Cut a lean piece of beef and add chopped parsley, spring onions, a bay leaf and cloves, a few small onions and slices of carrots, salt and pepper. In an ovenproof terrine place a layer of the beef mixture, a layer of bacon, and then season and repeat; at the end, add a spoonful of Calvados diluted with two spoonfuls of water. Close the terrine dish and bake in the oven for 5 to 6 hours, depending on the quantities.

Teurgoule

2l of milk, forty sugar cubes, one glass or 125g of rice and a little cinnamon depending on taste. That is all. Cook in the oven at a very low heat for about 4 hours.

Crèvecoeur chickens are also entitled to their own Normandy home.

Timber-framing enables all sorts of decorative fantasies: mosaic brickwork, small tile fragments, chequerboard.

Poulet sauté à la crème

Sauteed Chicken with Cream

Carve a chicken and brown the pieces in butter. When it is well browned, reduce the heat and add a little water to prevent it from sticking.

Add salt and pepper. When it is cooked, add about 50 centimes worth of thick cream and stir the sauce with one or two spoons. Add some finely chopped herbs and leave to heat gently on the corner of the stove.

Poires à la bonne femme

Pears à la Bonne Femme

Wash the pears in cold water without peeling them, then place them in a terrine with 50cl of water, a little cinnamon, twelve sugar cubes and seal the terrine and cook on a low heat. When the pears are half-cooked, add a glass of good red wine. When they are cooked, this wine must be almost completely reduced.

Place the pears in a bowl and remove the juice from the terrine with a spoonful of water and pour it over the pears. Serve hot or cold.

Teurgoule.

Escalopes de veau aux morilles à la crème

Veal Scallops with Creamy Morel Mushrooms

In Normandy, it is said that to be strong, it is necessary to eat veal at Ascension. Therefore, let us prepare scallops on that day. As for the morels, it is possible to find some here because of the limestone soil they appreciate so much.

Sear the scallops on both sides in oil and butter so that they are nicely browned. Pepper them and leave to cook for 5 mins, then add salt. Wash the morels and remove all the sand and dust.

Remove the scallops and keep them warm. Throw away the fat and add a little water in the frying pan and place on the stove. Add the morels, fresh cream, salt and pepper.

Put the scallops back in the pan and cook at a low heat for a further 10 mins.

Confiture de citrouille et de pommes

Pumpkin and Apple Jam

A 1kg pumpkin cut into cubes, five Rambault apples (a very acidic variety from the Pays d'Auge) and 600g of sugar for the above quantities. Leave to macerate overnight. They will release a great deal of water. Cook gently for 50 to 60 mins and pour into pots.

The interior of Champ-Versant is very typical of small manors of which there were dozens: narrow, because their width depended on the size of the lintel joining the two facades; often comprising two rooms separated by the vestibule, decorated here by a door with ionic pilasters and acanthus leaves; and embellished with huge fireplaces at each gable.

Gelée de pommes infaillible

Can't-Go-Wrong Apple Jelly

This is made at the end of September or in October with fruit which is not quite ripe. Windfalls give good results.

Quarter the apples (which enables them to be checked for worms. If they are damaged cut out the bad parts). Above all, do not peel them. Wash them and lay the quarters in an enamel or copper pot. Cover the apples with water and cook for 1 1/2 hours, then empty into a sieve or a linen cloth which is left suspended over a container big enough to catch the juice for 12 hours.

Madame Letrésor's grandmother used two chairs and bags of sugars as weights, put the apples in a tea towel and suspended it above a basin overnight.

Next, measure out the juice and add 500g of sugar for every litre; boil for 25 mins skimming regularly, then put into jars. After a few days, the jelly will have set. Cover in the same way as ordinary jam. The colourful fruit create a beautiful pink colour. Madame Letrésor makes a syrup with 2l of juice: 2 glasses of water, 1.5kg of sugar and says: «For a jelly to be successful, you must be able to read your newspaper through it.»

The trou normand

This section is a little as if we were at a large feast where each of our castles is a dish and where a break is taken to help digest what has been eaten and to exchange ideas: the Trou Normand. The *Robert* dictionary dates the expression from 1867, therefore, it is only natural that the Trou Normand does not appear at Madame Bovary's wedding meal ten years earlier: « The table was laid under the cart-shed [...] At the corners were decanters of brandy. Sweet bottled-cider frothed round the corks, and all the glasses had been filled to the brim with wine beforehand. Large dishes of yellow cream, that trembled with the least shake of the table, had designed on their smooth surface the initials of the newly wedded pair in nonpareil arabesques [...] », but brandy, especially when drunk down in one, was already known for its digestive virtues. But, it was not sipped, it was swallowed while people talked.

At this feast there will be some important guests, all great lovers of their province, bandying words which are sometimes tender and often cruel. They are known: Flaubert, Maupassant, Allais... they are Normans at heart and in character. They enjoy their food but know that the dining table is an important part of society life. The first speaker will be Jehan Le Hir, the founder of the « Tripe d'Or », who recounts in verse the adventure of Rouen-style Duckling, of which we will not forget this: « Stirring it over the flame with great diligence

Master seasons this dish, a dish full... of eloquence. »

Our connoisseurs of the good things in life applaud the Master and shout: « Gustave! Tell us about Boucharine once more! » And, as at every meal, Flaubert recounts the hilarious story of the recipe which should have made Bouvard and Pécuchet rich: somewhere between Caen and Falaise, this new liqueur containing coriander, kirsch, hyssop, umbrette,

In the library of Château de Sassy, L'architecture gastronomique *by Jules Gouffé.*

The rite of the woodcock by Guy de Maupassant. Because there is no good meal without good stories. And, Normans are masters in that domain.

colamus aromaticus, was going to replace Bénédictine from Fecamp. Alas! «The alembic exploded into twenty pieces, and the rounded part of the still was found bolted into the ceiling.» Everybody laughs at this story which has been heard so many times.

«Alright, I'll set up my woodcock.» It is Guy de Maupassant who is speaking. And repeating the rite which opens his «Contes de la Bécasse», he attaches one of the heads – because we have eaten woodcock – on a cork, the cork on a spinning knife and it is fate which will decide the happy winner of all the heads which, when grilled over a hot flame are a true treat for hunters. The head turns, then stops in front of Alphonse Allais, you know, the son of the chemist from Honfleur.

He is a prodigious teller of short stories, such as the one about the duck which ate the peas «with which he should have been served», or the one about the old marquis who was made to eat his collection of beans. Or even, the one about the discovery of the cold meat quarries («pork, this useful assistant of the butcher»). He concludes with a recipe of his own:

« Tout d'abord pigeons
Sept ou huit pigeons!
Aux doux veaux rognons
Leur tenders rognons,
Qu'alors nous oginons
Du jus des oignons!
Puis, enfin, bondons
Vous de gras bondons!
Les vins? Avalons
D'exquis Avallons! »

(Bravo, bravo) «Another, another!» But, it is Maupassant's turn to recount some crude stories about the Pays de Caux. Then Flaubert asks for spinach. Why spinach? «It is the stomach's broom». We recognise well his Dictionnaire des Idées Recues. But it is time to head out into the night, leaving behind this joyous gathering which proves, if need be, that Normans are not always as quiet as they are said to be.

MANOIR DE SAINT-HIPPOLYTE

An agricultural manor

Would the owners of this old manor not be the beautiful Norman cows which produce rich milk and delicious cheeses? The many activities put forward by the estate are centred around the farm: a preserved site with orchards, a press, an alembic, a dovecote, hives and a modern cheese factory. All these buildings surround a 16th century manor, the ground floor of which is built in limestone with the upper floors in Saint-Jean stone and bricks and timber-framed dormers: all the materials from the Pays d'Auge are brought together here, even the floor slabs in Pré d'Auge in the monumental halls. The hexagonal dovecote is also built on a stone base, a protection against damp from the river. In former times, on this bank of the Touques, a river famed for its trout which are caught by fly-fishing, and which ends by separating Trouville from Deauville, there used to be a Gallo-Roman villa. This was followed by a feudal mound and moats. The bread oven is proof that this used to be an ordinary fief while the dovecote shows that it was a seigniory. Today, it is a showcase for Norman agriculture. Naturally, the recipes we present here are faithful to their region.

Top.
The manor's metal plate.
Opposite.
The castle seen from the bottom with the dovecote on the left.

At the top of its terrace, the manor, with well-balanced proportions, watches over the little world of its Norman courtyard.

The Normandy breed, which mixes Nordic and local origins, is old nobility: its Herd-Book, listing filiations, dates back to 1883 and is one of the first in France. It is mixed race, bred for its meat as well as for its rich and creamy milk.

TOURNEDOS DE BŒUF À LA CRÈME DE COLONEL

Beef Tournedos with Colonel's Cream

For 4 people
1 250g colonel,
1l of single cream,
4 Normandy AOC beef filet tournedos,
10g of butter.

« Colonel » is the other name for Livarot, owing to the five stripes which encircle it, the same as a colonel's stripes.

Melt the Livarot in the single cream, blend together and season. Keep warm while cooking the tournedos. Sear the beef fillets in butter. Add salt and pepper and serve them rare. Coat them with colonel's sauce and serve with a Gratin Dauphinois and some French beans.

Salmis of Pigeon with Pommeau

SALMIS DE PIGEON AU POMMEAU

Salmis of Pigeon with Pommeau

For 2 people

1 600g pigeon,
1 chopped onion,
2 diced carrots,
1 stick of celery,
3 strands of parsley,
4 large button mushrooms,
8 firm potatoes such as Charlotte,
50g of white flour,
20cl of Pommeau,
50cl of vegetable stock,
20cl of peanut oil,
20g of butter.

In a thick-bottomed cocotte, sear the pigeon in the oil and butter, then remove and fry the onions, carrots, celery and parsley. Flambé the Pommeau and add 50g of flour, soak with the vegetable stock and add the pigeon, potatoes, mushrooms and leave to cook over a low heat for 45 mins. Serve the pigeon medium-rare with the potatoes and mushrooms.

Pavé d'Auge, Pont-l'Evêque and Livarot bearing the manor's label and the reeds, called «laîches», which are used to tie up the Livarot.

Tourte au livarot et au pont-l'Évêque

Livarot and Pont-l'Evêque Pie

Recipe by the Syndicate of Pont-l'Evêque manufacturers.

1/2 a Livarot,
1 Pont-l'Evêque,
250g of shortcrust pastry,
1 egg yolk,
10cl of fresh cream,
1 glass of milk,
pepper,
nutmeg,
20g of butter for the mould.

Remove the crust from both cheeses and chop them into small pieces. Whisk together the egg yolk, cream, milk, cheese, pepper and grated nutmeg. Turn on the oven to Gas N° 8. Roll out the pastry and place in a buttered pie dish. Pour the mixture on it and bake for 20 mins. Serve warm.

Top.
One of the timber-framed dormers, a typical construction method in the Pays d'Auge.

Right.
Brotherhoods, of which there are about twenty in Normandy, include those of Livarot and Pont-l'Evêque, which defend two origin-certified cheeses (six AOC exist in Normandy: Camembert, Pavé d'Auge, Livarot, Pont-l'Evêque, the butter and cream of Isigny). The Livarot brotherhood, on the left in the photo, was created in 1989. The aim of the brotherhood is to develop the reputation of the Pays d'Auge and to encourage appreciation for genuine Livarot from Normandy. The yearly chapter is held on the second Saturday in May. The brotherhood of the Knights of Pont-l'Evêque, on the right in the photo, was created in 1985 in order to promote one of the oldest cheeses in Normandy, given the name of this town of character in 1600, which encountered its first success with the development of the railway line which put Paris a short distance from Normandy. The chapter is held in October. These two brotherhoods are regulars at Festivals in Saint-Hippolyte.

SASSY

Under the watchful eyes of Vatel

The library in the Château de Sassy contains 10,000 books on all sorts of subjects; theology, political and natural science, literature, fine arts, etc. which can be found with the help of indexes on the two stories of shelving. All that an honest 19th century man needed to know. Etienne-Denis Pasquier, the son of a lawyer of Louis XVI, guillotined in 1794, was Councillor of State, Minister, Duke and member of the Academy. On his death at the age of 97, the title passed to a grand-nephew whom he had adopted, Edme-Armand-Gaton d'Audiffret, from an old family from Italy and Provence. Since then, the castle has stayed in the family, as well as the large forest and agricultural estate which surrounds it. Seen from below, Sassy is an imposing castle, which dominates the surrounding countryside from its northern façade. But, from it interior courtyard, at the crossroads of the forest alleyways lined with huge Corsican pines, it looks like a beautiful residence with one return wing breaking the symmetry. Started in 1760, it was completed by Chancellor Pasquier, who bought it in 1850, later adding its T-shaped wing and a French-style garden, which is only seen properly from the castle.
In the library, we consulted a few years of Denis d'Audiffret-Pasquier's hunting book: in the space of fifteen years (really fourteen because there was no hunting in 1870), 3,032 items of natural game, rabbit, quail, thrush, partridge and a few other species which are no longer hunted, were caught. It is not surprising then that the kitchen is so big!

Chantal rings the bell for lunch in Sassy's private kitchen.

The recipes of Count Lastic Saint-Jal

Sassy's library continues in its kitchens. Here we found several publications, in particular, this *Cuisine usuelle, recette culinaires, remèdes pratiques* by Lastic Saint-Jal, Madame d'Audiffret's grandfather, from which these recipes for game and other quadrupeds were taken.

GIGOT DE CHEVREUIL

Leg of Venison

« In order to eat good venison, it has to killed with a gun; an overstrained deer which dies of apoplexy has a bad taste and its flesh is tinged with blood. The front part of venison is eaten in a civet; the heart and liver with a spicy sauce. The blood is eaten in an omelette by hunters who appreciate this, but, in reality, the reputation of venison comes from the fillets and legs. »

Trim a leg of venison, removing all its skin and fibres, and marinate for 24 hours in olive oil with sliced onions, bay leaves, thyme and garlic turning it several times.

Often, venison is marinated in wine, or in vinegar but this is a not a good idea because it decomposes the meat and gives it an unpleasant taste; therefore, use oil only and do not salt the meat which drains its juices. In order to roast it, place the leg of venison over a hot fire and coat it regularly with its marinade which you have strained.

Salt the roast 10 mins before removing from the heat. Eat with a spicy sauce, known as a Venison sauce. It is made as follows: Make a roux with butter and flour. Add finely chopped shallots taking care not to let them brown. Soak with stock and add four cloves of garlic cooked in the cinders and crushed, salt, pepper, nutmeg, a bunch of parsley, a bay leaf and as much vinegar as is needed to make the sauce acidulous. Cook for 1/2 an hour. Strain the sauce and 5 mins before serving add capers or chopped gherkins.

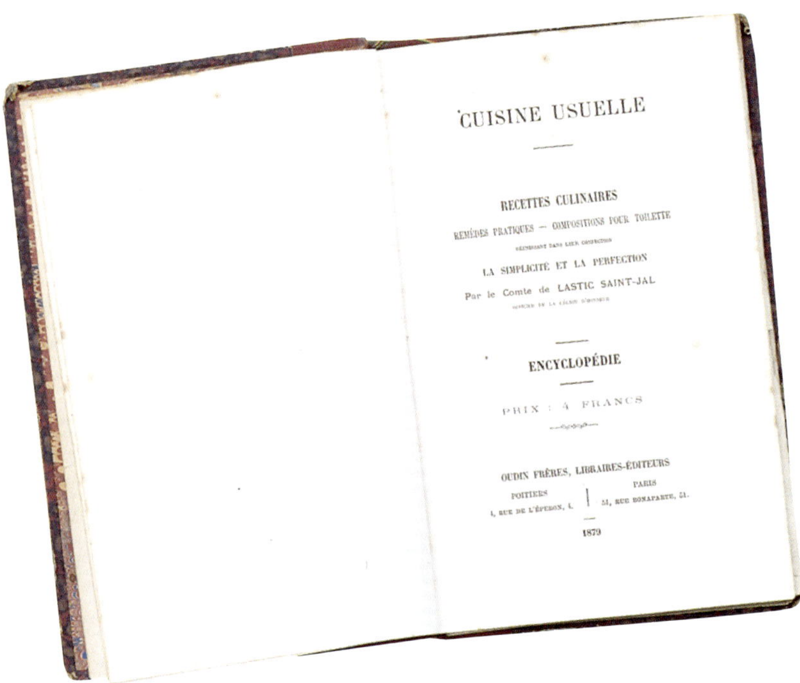

CUISINE USUELLE

RECETTES CULINAIRES

REMÈDES PRATIQUES — COMPOSITIONS POUR TOILETTE

LA SIMPLICITÉ ET LA PERFECTION

Par le Comte de LASTIC SAINT-JAL

ENCYCLOPÉDIE

PRIX : 4 FRANCS

OUDIN FRÈRES, LIBRAIRES-ÉDITEURS

POITIERS
4, RUE DE L'ÉPERON, 4.

PARIS
51, RUE BONAPARTE, 51.

1879

GIBIER À PLUMES

Feathered Game

« Among the large number of indigenous birds which take pride of place on gourmets' tables, pheasant and partridge are the main ones. Among some of the more exotic birds which arrive in France at certain times of the year, woodcock, quail and snipe play an important role in gastronomy.

In France, we have indigenous birds which have an excellent reputation, but they are so rare and so uncommon that it is necessary to allow those who live in the areas privileged with the presence of grouse, capercaillie, hazel grouse the worry of how to prepare them... Quail is fat after the harvest, thrush after the grape harvest and the skylark in autumn.

Each of these birds, therefore, has its own time when it offers up its culinary qualities and if it is not taken in season it is very different from what you find when eaten at the right time of year.

The thrush and the skylark should not be emptied and, in order to prepare an excellent roast, they should be barded with fresh bacon and roasted at a high heat. Small game, if kept too long on a skewer, dries out and loses its fumet. Pieces of bread are placed in the dripping pan to catch what falls from the roast. A true salmis is generally prepared with game. First choice is woodcock, snipe and quail; then comes wild duck, teal, plover, peewit, waterfowl, thrush, skylark, corncrake and others too numerous to name... Wild duck is better, in terms of quality of flesh and finesse of taste, compared to the domesticated duck; nevertheless the species must not be confused because there are several categories in this large family.

Wild duck, which resembles the domestic duck in size and plumage, is the only one which should be chosen; the merganser, the widgeon and many others have a mediocre taste and their flesh is oily or musky. When the wild duck is young, it is called halbran and is greatly sought after by gourmets. Wild duck is eaten in different ways. It is very good roasted when it is fat and, above all if it is cooked at a high temperature for half an hour, in the same way as it is eaten in Normandy. Teal is very fine and is prepared in the same way as wild duck; the same as for domesticated duck. Roast duck is eaten on a bed of watercress or on toasted pieces of bread. »

Jules Gouffé (1807-1877), a disciple of Carême, one of the best chefs in the 19th century, was nicknamed « the apostle of decorative cuisine ». Cuisine as a form of fine art...

The portrait of Vatel.

«A quite magnificent castle: composite but which has always been transformed with the purpose of grandeur and noblesse.» To this quote by La Varende, we will add the feeling of amicable familiarity emitted by this façade in the light of the setting sun.

«... See Chantal, she knows the house as well as I do. She will tell you everything you need to know.» The Duchess of Audiffret set the tone for this house of trust and serenity. In the small universe of her kitchen, Chantal has enjoyed the trust of her employers and has assured quality for the past twenty years. It is a kitchen where there is life and where her children grew up. She has seen many prestigious banquets and many more family meals. The large cast-iron oven is no longer used, although it was still in service in 1967 when Queen Elizabeth II stayed there, but she now has a gas oven and a wood oven if needed. Her castle kitchen is large and well-lit. One side faces south while the other side faces the front of the castle where there is a serving bell to inform that meals are ready. Around it are various storage rooms and cellars. A dumb-waiter leads to the pantry on the upper floor which serves the castle's private dining room and the ceremonial dining room, dominated by a portrait of Vatel: this famous maître d'hôtel of the Prince of Condé killed himself on 24 April 1671: he had prepared a large meal, but the tide was late and he could not tolerate the dishonour of having a meal spoilt! Fortunately, cooks no longer kill themselves. But, this portrait reminds us that a well-made meal served at the right time is always a masterpiece, regardless of the setting.

Menu of 27 November

Pheasant Terrine
Guinea Fowl with Grapes
Cheese
Rhubarb Pie

This year's Sassy Cider
Last year's Sassy Cider

Pintade aux raisins

Guinea Fowl with Raisins

Carve the guinea fowl and brown in a mixture of butter and oil. When well browned, flambé with a glass of Calvados and add a bottle of cider. Chantal says, «I add two bay leaves, salt and pepper and leave to stew. When it is cooked, I add the raisins which I have soaked in hot water. I use two sorts of raisins to provide two different colours. When cooked, I thicken with 20g of cornflour and just before serving I add two spoonfuls of fresh cream. I serve this dish with small round steamed potatoes.» Preparing the small potatoes generates a great deal of peel which can be fried to make amusing shapes for children.

Pie de rhubarbe du potager

Rhubarb Pie

Cut the rhubarb into pieces and remove any tough strands. Place in an ovenproof terrine dish and sprinkle with caster sugar; coat the sides with egg yolk mixed with water to stick the edges of the puff pastry which covers the terrine. Cut a hole in the middle and create a chimney with tinfoil. Glaze the pastry with egg yolk diluted with a little milk or water. Cook for 45 mins in a medium oven. Serve warm or cold in its dish with fresh single cream and allow guests to add sugar according to taste.

The pantry in the Château de Sassy. It is the central point for faultless service.

CROQUETTES D'ŒUFS DURS

Hard-Boiled Egg Croquettes

Make a very thick white sauce, cook the eggs, dice them and mix with the white sauce. Oil a dish and spread the mixture in it and leave to cool in the fridge. Remove when well chilled. Cut into the shape of a cork and dip in a beaten egg and then in breadcrumbs. Put back in the fridge so that the breadcrumbs stick. Fry for a few minutes just before serving.

BOUDIN BLANC

White Pudding

Dice six large white onions and cook them in hot water. Then fry them in a saucepan with 500g of lard without letting them brown. Chop and grind some lard, the same amount of spit-roasted chicken, especially the white meat, If this meat is not available, use veal or pork. Add the same quantity of bread as meat with the crusts removed soaked in cream or milk. Mix together with six egg yolks, salt, nutmeg, white pepper, a quart of fresh cream. Pour into the saucepan with the onions. Now that the mixture is ready, place it into tripe skin and cook in lightly boiling water for a 1/2 of an hour.

GRENADINS DE VEAU À L'OSEILLE

Grenadine of Veal with Sorrel

« Veal is an excellent food which is very useful in cooking, but in order to eat good quality veal it should be taken while six weeks or two months old and still feeding from its mother; later, when it starts to eat it becomes a store calf and its flesh is tough and its taste is less delicate than that of milk-fed veal. » (Lustic Saint-Jal)

The grenadines are cut in the same way as scallops but are not so wide and are thicker, similar to tournedos. They are taken from the cushion of veal and, generally, they are spiked with fine lardons. Sear the grenadines in a mixture of oil and butter over a hot flame until browned on both sides. Remove the meat, throw away the fat and add 20cl of white wine. Leave on the hot flame until the wine has reduced and add the grenadines and a little stock so that the meat is immersed by half; reduce the heat, and add salt and pepper. Cover and leave to stew for about 45 mins. During this time, chop a large bouquet of sorrel which has been washed and with the stalks removed. Melt some butter in a small high-sided frying pan and cook the sorrel over a low heat.

When the grenadines are cooked, lay the sorrel on a plate and place the grenadines on top and keep warm. Reduce the sauce further and add cream. Pour over the dish.

PETITS SABLÉS AUX ŒUFS DURS

Small Hard-Boiled Egg Shortbread Biscuits

150g of flour,
100g of butter,
75g of granulated sugar,
the yolks of 2 hard-boiled eggs,
a little salt,
the zest of one lemon.

Put the flour in the bowl and form a well into which you will place all the other ingredients. Knead the dough with the two hard-boiled egg yolks which have been sieved and the melted butter. Form a ball, and leave to cool, especially in the summer when the dough is soft because of the large amount of butter. When the dough is firm, roll it out relatively thickly. Cut out the biscuit shapes. Cook in a very hot oven on a buttered oven tray for 5 to 6 mins.

Pudding du cabinet

Bathroom Pudding

Recipe by Madame de Blanchy, Madame d'Audiffret-Pasquier's mother. This pudding was nicknamed « bathroom pudding » by the children. In effect, when it was prepared, the cake was rolled in a linen cloth and was placed in the bathroom bidet for the night, because the bidet was the only object in the house long enough to accommodate the pudding!

1kg of raisins, 1kg of currants, 2 quarters of citron, the zest of 4 lemons, 1kg of granulated sugar, half a glass of brandy, half a grated nutmeg. Mix these ingredients together in advance and leave overnight.

500g of bread with the crusts removed, 500g of flour, 1kg of very fresh beef marrow, 18 eggs, milk. Add all of these ingredients the day of cooking. Mix all the ingredients together well; place the mixture in a cloth dampened with hot water and sprinkle with flour, or, if you want it to darken, spread some butter on the cloth before sprinkling with flour.

Cook in a bain-marie for 6 hours. Stir a little so that the raisins do not sink to the bottom.

The dining room in the Château de Sassy.

Carrouges

Hunters and hunting

A hunting air accompanied our visit to this large castle surrounded by its moats on the edge of Ecouves Forest. But, we will not limit Carrouges to its hunting and fishing festival, for this castle is linked to a very ancient legend: the story of Ralph, the lord of the castle, who, when out hunting one day, encountered a fairy with whom he fell in love. Of his pregnant wife who killed the fairy. Of Ralph again found the next day with his throat cut. Of his posthumous son Karl le Rouge, wearing a bloodstain on his forehead in atonement for murder. When the Carrouges family died out, the estate passed to the Blosset family, which undertook major works, then to the Le Veneur family, the King's hunters, until 1936 when the castle, by then in a very poor state of repair, was bought by the State along with a large part of its furniture… a little by chance according to the castle's brochure. Although Carrouges has been open to the public since before the War, forty years were needed to repair the roofs. Now a public monument, Carrouges has not lost any of its charm and soul. We were lucky to have been there on a beautiful day, received by the staff and the castle's administrator Claude-Catherine Terrier, in order to find some delicious recipes from this land of game and good food which symbolise Karl le Rouge, Diana and Actaeon.

Top.
«…she gave the horns of a mature stag to the head she had sprinkled, lengthening his neck, making his ear-tips pointed, changing feet for hands, long legs for arms…» This chest in an upstairs antechamber tells the story of Actaeon who, having surprised Diana bathing with her nymphs, was turned into a stag and devoured by his hounds.
Opposite.
The castle's bakery is remarkable for the stone vault of the fireplace with its four ovens.

A very local dish

« La petite oie »

This is a special «civet» which is popular at Christmas and New Year. It comprises the offal from the goose destined for roasting and uses the pinions, neck, feet (boiled and peeled), gizzard, heart and kidneys.

Everything is browned in a large cast-iron pot with butter and oil and singed ever so slightly.

Add a large quantity of chopped onions and sliced carrot as well as celery sticks and a traditional bouquet garni: parsley, bay leaf, thyme and a few cloves. Pepper and salt.

Add a salted pork trotter cut into pieces. Soak with cold water so that it is barely covered and cook on a very low heat for several hours.

It is served traditionally with Soissons beans cooked separately in water with salt and a bouquet garni. These may be replaced by chestnuts or chestnuts with Soissons beans.

It is important that this dish is not a simple stew but a civet, therefore the sauce should be thickened at the end with the goose's blood. Mix the blood with a few spoonfuls of gravy before pouring it into the pot and mixing it all together with a wooden spoon.

If the goose's blood is not available, it can be replaced with blood from a rabbit or a pig. But, if possible, try to use goose only.

It is so good that it is worthwhile using the whole goose, or at least the poorest cuts.

Right page.
The small entrance castle: richly decorated with black brick and red brick diamonds. It is Gothic but bears a suggestion of the Renaissance.

Below.
A large quadrilateral surrounded by moats, balustrades and railings: a castle set in the plain, Carrouges built some imposing defences.

Coat-of-arms of the Le Veneur family in silver with an azure strip inset with gold and the motto: «I like it as it is».

Below.

«Through this marriage, the land of Carrouges was transferred to the Le Veneur family in around 1500.» This inscription appears on the double portrait of Philippe Le Veneur and his wife Marie Blosset, Baroness de Tillières and daughter of the lord of Carrouges, which dominates the two fountains in the dining room. On the table, the centrepiece belonging to the Republican, General Alexis Le Veneur, Count of the Empire and the person responsible for building Carrouge's large banquet hall.

Petits farcis impromptus « de la Marquise »

The Marquise's Small Stuffing Surprises

Some good fatty rillettes – goose, rabbit or duck, even pork, it is not important – from which you will remove the fat (1.2kg of rillettes for 12 stuffing surprises). To do this, heat and «drain» the cooked flesh*. Mix with chopped onion which has been browned in a frying pan, a little cream, two chopped hard-boiled eggs and finely ground toast, and perfume with a drop of Calvados. Do not forget to add some parsley or chives, pepper and a little salt.

Place a good soup-spoon of this stuffing in some puff pastry or even – if necessary – bread dough, and cut out small shapes and glaze them with egg.

Place in a well-heated oven for about 20 mins.

Everything can be prepared in 1/2 of an hour. This preparation can also be used to stuff small pieces of feathered game. Also, the hot mixture is ideal for filling a quick omelette. It can also be served inside a buckwheat pancake and is delicious for a quick snack when served on toast.

The small surprises are served in the salon after the performance.

The Marquise of Verdelin, born de Brémont d'Ars was the mother-in-law of General Alexis Paul Michel Le Veneur de Tillières. She was one of the patrons of Jean-Jacques Rousseau with whom she maintained a correspondence.

The terrace garden.

A friend of the Arts and Letters, at Carrouges, she was also the instigator of the castle's imposing theatre where the General himself performed.

*The modern version consists of placing the rillettes on a plate between two sheets of absorbent paper and putting them in the microwave oven for 2-3 minutes. All the fat is absorbed by the paper. Preferably, take rillettes with firm pieces of meat.

The Marquise's small stuffing surprises, here presented on a plate belonging to the Le Veneur family.

Top.
Death of a stag, painting by Jules Gélibert.

Côtelettes de chevreuil Le Veneur

Le Veneur Venison Chops

In very hot butter sauté four chops for each guest. Keep warm in the open oven. Deglaze the cooking dish with a small glass of Calvados, scrape the bottom of the dish and flambé. If you wish, add a few crushed juniper berries.
Add a large quantity of thick cream and «cook» until it has reduced by half. Add a teaspoon of good cider vinegar, ground pepper and salt.
Add the juices from the dish and, if you wish, a little redcurrant jelly.

Pour the sauce over the chops presented on a very hot serving dish. Serve with a dry timbale of acidic apple purée.

Bronze by P.J. Même, end of the 19th century; the beater covers the forest before the hunt with a branch in his hand to mark his path. At the meeting point of Ecouves and Andaines, two large nationally owned forests, every year, Carrouges plays host to a famous hunting festival.

Quite simply

Côtes de sanglier à la cheminée

Fire-Grilled Chops of Wild Boar

Plenty of embers, thick chops (fresh or frozen).

Cook on the grill for about 3 mins on each side depending on whether you like them rare or more well-done. Salt, pepper, cranberry sauce. With potatoes baked in the cinders, wrapped in tinfoil, or a celery purée and a good salad to which you will add a diced apple.

In this same antechamber there are still the remains of a rich decoration bearing the coat-of-arms of the Le Veneur family, such as this hunting scene dating from the 16th century over the fireplace.

Top.
The interior courtyard gives unity to the castle built over two centuries, with the Blosset family's wing in the background.

Bottom.
The Le Veneur family was also masters of the Forges and surrounded their castle with « real iron » rails, practically indestructible.

TERRINE DE POMMES AU PAIN D'ÉPICE

Apple Terrine with Gingerbread

A large oven dish is needed (for example 20 x 30 cm and 5 cm high). Cover the bottom with a layer of slices (1 cm) of good gingerbread – artisanal gingerbread is best (about 250g). Cover this with a glassful of good Calvados (about 10cl). You will need about 2kg of apples, preferably not too sweet (russets are ideal). Peel them, trim them, quarter them and then cut them into thin slices.

Cover the gingerbread with a layer of apple, a few drops of lemon juice,

some small pieces of half-salted butter, and sprinkle with the brown sugar (almost five soup-spoons is needed, namely 100g).

Continue with another layer of apple, lemon, butter, sugar. In total, there should be several layers of apple (about five or six layers).

Cook in a pre-heated oven at 180° for slightly over 1 hour. The top should be lightly caramelised. It can be protected with greaseproof paper to finish it.

This dish may be eaten hot, warm with a bowl of fresh cream or cold with fruit jelly: quince, raspberry, etc.

The kitchen is in the old part of the castle where the buildings come together against the moat. It was completed by a greenhouse for fruit, a bakery, a chicken coop, wine cellars and a dining room for servants. On the table, a traditional wooden cider jug and on the sideboard a mill for grinding buckwheat.

Bonneville

For the love of a house

« Dionysus should have been one of the great French patrons who would have had his home between Dijon and Chagny, a cathedral in Gironde and his chapel in Reims. » The person who wrote that, Jean Mallard, Count of La Varende, well deserved his place in *La Cuisine des Châteaux*. A political writer launched by the success of *Nez-de-Cuir*, he prided himself on only writing about true facts. It is surprising to read the lively and sometimes brutal style of this writer and chronicler, a traditional rightwing man and monarchist, nostalgic for a bygone golden age. He was born in Bonneville in 1887, studied in Rennes, which he did not like very much, and returned to Bonneville to be at one with his home as a modest squireling: « I am my leading valet, I admit it entirely. I shut the house every evening in the same way as if kissing a child who has touched your heart. » He knew the limits of that which was « no more than a charming home », near the enormous castle of the Princes of Broglie, a son of whom later married his granddaughter. But he took care of it in the same way as an artisan: from him, the rosace made with bread which still surrounds the chandelier in the dining room, from him the woodwork, furniture and paintings, from him the oratory on to which opens a cupboard in the dining room, from him the miniature cannon which mocks visitors from the corner of the stairs. And, finally, from him an extraordinary collection of model boats. Not having travelled himself, Jean de La Varende recreated ships meticulously in his attic, and as he did with every surprising fact in his life, he wrote a book about it in which legendary ships succeed one another. La Varende's cuisine is in perfect harmony with the personage: here, the Shepherd's Pie served the second day of the Pot-au-Feu, is called the civil burial... The writer was buried in 1959. His daughter-in-law, Brigitte de La Varende, who opens the gardens to visitors showed us the recipe books of this family home: « It is a much loved house which is growing old with grace. »

Chou farci aux marrons

Cabbage stuffed with Chestnuts

For 7 or 8 people

1 firm white cabbage which weighs about 1.5kg when peeled,
6 onions together weighing 200g,
500g of chestnuts,
225g at least of butter,
30cl of very good milk, namely about a glass and a half,
15g of salt,
4g of ground pepper.
Time required: 2 hours to prepare the stuffing and the cabbage and 5 hours for cooking.

The chestnuts

It is necessary to start with them because they take the longest to cook. Always choose very good quality chestnuts, meaning well-rounded with a tender and shiny skin and a good size. They must not be left whole but they must also not be crushed into a paste. Only remove the first skin completely. Place them in a saucepan and cover with cold water. Put a lid on the pan and boil for a quarter of an hour at a medium heat. At this point, the second skin comes off very easily and the chestnut does not break. Remove the skin with a small knife and add the chestnuts to the onions which you have prepared in the meantime.

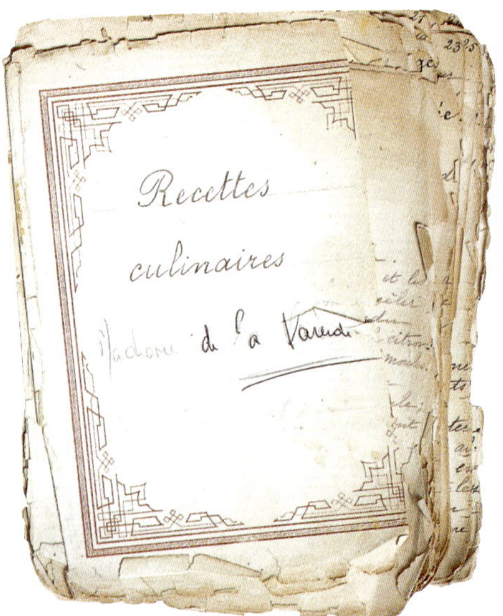

The onions and stuffing: peel the onions and slice them finely. Choose a deep, thick copper pan the same size as the cabbage. Remember that the cabbage must be a tight fit but that during cooking it will reduce in size. However, it would be no problem to prepare the onion stuffing in a different pan. Put the onion slices and a large egg-sized piece of butter in the pan. Stir over a low heat to melt and mix together. Cover the saucepan and the onions to reduce slowly without browning. Once the onions are ready, add the carefully peeled chestnuts. Also, add the rest of the butter once you have set aside 50g to use later on. Cover the pan again and leave to simmer at a low heat stirring regularly with a wooden spoon. Be careful not to crush the chestnuts into a paste. They should break up into pieces, but the pieces should remain intact. Gradually, everything will start to brown. Count a good half-hour of cooking at a very low heat so that the chestnuts absorb the butter and become caramelised, the same colour as candied chestnuts. Add half the salt as well as the pepper. Then empty on to a plate along with all the fat left by the butter.

The cabbage

Cut the base from the cabbage on a level with the leaves. Remove any damaged leaves and any which are still green. Have a large saucepan of boiling water ready. Put the cabbage in the water with the base facing downwards. The entire cabbage should be covered in the boiling water. Cover and bring to the boil and continue to boil until the leaves no longer break when they are handled. This usually takes half an hour. Strain the cabbage and place it in cold water then squeeze it between both hands to remove all the water. Place it on a large, clean tea towel and unfold the leaves one by one spreading them out on the cloth, but not separating them. Continue until you reach the last leaves which you are unable to unfold. Place a small amount of stuffing on this small arrangement of leaves. Place a leaf over this leaf and spread a small amount of stuffing. Fold over the next leaf and continue always being sure to place the stuffing in the centre of cabbage in order to give it back its original shape. Once all the leaves have been folded back into position, surround the cabbage with a string passed twice around it in the shape of a cross and tie the ends together on the top of the cabbage leaving the ends long enough to be able to lift it out of the pan. With your fingers, spread the remaining butter around the pan. Place the cabbage in the pan with its base facing downwards. Sprinkle with the remaining salt and pepper. Cover and place on a low heat. Once it has started simmering and the butter has melted and is hot, count 5 hours of cooking time. Uncover from time to time to baste the cabbage with the cooking juices but do not turn it over. Always remember to cover and ensure that it does not stick when you move it. Half-way through the cooking time, add the milk which you have kept, but keep a few spoonfuls behind to thin the gravy a quarter of an hour before serving. Continue basting about three times every hour.

Serving

Untie the string. Place on a round and hot plate, pour the juice around it and take care to use the brown skin which has formed on the side of the pan during cooking. This recipe is long, but no more than the preparation required. Now you know how to make stuffed cabbage!

Most of the comments here are taken from this small little-known book.

CHARTREUSE DE FAISAN OU DE PERDRIX

Chartreuse of Pheasant or Partridge

For a large pheasant, or two partridges, take three Savoy cabbages, ten average-sized carrots, ten turnips, two sausages, a few pieces of bacon, a few slices of dried sausage. Cook your pheasant in advance in gravy or roux and prepare enough sauce. Add the cabbages chopped in two or in four depending on their size, then the small slices of bacon and the sausages. Slice the carrots and turnips. Cook in boiling water with a little butter and a pinch of sugar and salt. Carve your pheasant, cut your sausages into slices. Once the garnish is cooked and ready, take a mould and butter it well. Place a layer of carrots and turnips in the bottom, then a layer of cabbage, pieces of pheasant, a layer of cabbage, one of sausage and another of dried sausage; continue to alternate adding a spoonful of sauce. When your mould is almost full (2cm from the top), place it in a bain-marie and cook for an hour. When serving, remove it from its mould and surround it with the sauce. Serve very hot.

Note: if you do not have a partridge or a pheasant, you can also use pigeon but it would require longer cooking time.

LES RÉPUBLICAINS

Republicans

500g of flour,
375g of butter,
200g of sugar,
a pinch of salt,
a little milk.

When your pastry is ready, roll it out. Cut out your cakes and sprinkle with sugar. Cook in a very hot oven for about 10 mins.

LES ARISTOCRATES

Aristocrats

125g of butter, 125g of sugar, 250g of flour, a little ground vanilla, one egg. Make a pastry with all the ingredients. Roll out very thin. Cut out small sticks. Decorate with a mixture of egg white and icing sugar whisked until a smooth paste is obtained. This is called royal icing. Cook on a baking tray. Keep an eye on them while cooking, no more than 15 mins in general.

UN RÊVE

A dream

Six eggs, with the whites stiffened, 125g of crushed dried macaroons and a little caster sugar. Mix all the ingredients together keeping the egg yolks aside. Pour into a mould glazed with caramel. Cook for 1 hour in a bain-marie. Serve with a vanilla custard prepared with the egg yolks.

Gâteau aux carottes

Carrot Cake

500g of sugar, 500g of finely grated almonds, two soup-spoons of flour, 500g of carrots boiled in water and sieved, four egg yolks, a small glass of kirsch.

Mix everything together for half an hour and then add the stiffened egg whites. Butter a mould and bake the cake for 45 mins.

When it has cooled, ice it with sugar and kirsch or with jam sprinkled with grated almonds.

Carrot cake. Here in the dining room where Jean de La Varende created a small oratory in one of the corner towers.

Quatre-quarts à l'orange

Orange Pound Cake

Put 125g of granulated sugar and two eggs in a bowl and add a little orange or lemon zest. Whisk for about 5 mins until you have obtained a white creamy mixture with small bubbles, then sieve in 125g of flour. Mix for another 5 mins. Add 125g of melted butter, mix and pour into a flat, well-buttered cake tin. Bake at a low heat for 30 mins. Turn out and leave to cool.

Confiture de prunes d'avoine

White Primordian Plum Jam

For a basket of plums, 2kg of granulated sugar and four glasses of water. In the bottom of the cauldron, place an upside down plate with a hole in it, the water, the plums and the sugar in layers and cook for 10 hours. It is essential to use White Primordian plums (which is the main difficulty of the recipe!). This jam is made in September.

Tôt-fait

125g of flour,
125g of sugar,
125g of buttter,
2 or 3 eggs,
1 grated lemon,
75g of currants.

Whisk together the sugar and the eggs, add the flour and the warm melted butter, currants and lemon. Butter and flour small cake moulds. Put a spoonful of mixture in each mould. Cook in a medium oven for 20 mins.

Marquis

In a bowl, prepare six bars of grated chocolate and 300g of fresh butter. Boil two glasses of milk, 200g of granulated sugar, half a vanilla pod. When it has boiled, pour the mixture gradually over six egg yolks and keep on a low heat, without letting it boil, until it thickens. Use a spoon to pour it gradually over the chocolate and butter mixture prepared earlier and pour the mixture into a mould filled with sponge biscuits. The biscuits should be placed upright around the inside of the mould. Cover with the cream and then with finish with the biscuits. Cover the mould pressing down well and leave to cool until the next day.

Gâteaux Saint-Pierre

Saint Peter's Cake

400g of flour, 300g of sugar, 300g of butter, a pinch of salt, two egg yolks. Roll out the pastry to the thickness of one finger and cut out diamond shapes scored with a knife, glaze with egg yolk and a little water. Bake for 10 mins in a cool oven.

Seen from this side, Bonneville resembles a small fortress. The moats have disappeared but the corner towers and lions from China remain. In the background, the castle's orangery.

Left page.
The orange pound cake on a wedding chest. Service bearing the La Varende initials.

DAPIBVS MENSAS ONERAMV

ANET

Diane's Mausoleum

On the table in the dining room of Château d'Anet stands a Renaissance vessel containing many symbols: the sovereign's objects, containers of spices from distant shores and «tests», or rather antidotes. The monumental fireplace bears the coat-of-arms of Diana and this inscription: «Dapidus mensas orneramus inemptis» (We fill our tables with food which is not bought). The pride of a castle is also to be self-sufficient.

The final chapter in the chequered life of Diane de Poitiers, one of our great courtesans, was played out at Anet. She retired here on the death of her King and after falling out of favour with Catherine de Medici. The changing winds of history dispersed her glory and Diane's mausoleums scatter the park at Anet.

Originally, there was a fortified castle, and later a huge home owned by the lords of Brézé. In 1515, Louis de Brézé, an important hunter in France, took a second wife, the 16-year old Diane de Poitiers. Beautiful, intelligent, a hunting enthusiast – and widowed in 1531, she became a conquest of Prince Henry, crowned Henry II in 1547. He gave her Chenonceau, which she decorated with their entwined monograms. Later, at Anet, these marks became an obsession after the death of the king in a tournament in 1559. Driven from Chenonceau and from the Queen's court, Diane mourned her lover even as far as in the decoration of the castle and the chapel.

In the Revolution, Anet was partially destroyed and sold several times before being saved by Ferdinand Moreau, a politician from whom descends the Yturbe family which occupies the castle today and has restored it. Anet is one of the most beautiful Renaissance monuments in France around the tomb of Diane who has returned to her park.

The recipes of Château d'Anet

as told by Michelle, the castle's cook

Lapin chasseur

Hunter's Rabbit

1 large rabbit,
200g of bacon,
200g of mushrooms,
1 onion,
200g of small carrots,
1 glass of dry white wine,
20 small potatoes (ratte).

Cut the rabbit into pieces and brown in butter. Deglaze with white wine. Add the blanched lardons and the chopped onions. Then, add the small carrots and mushrooms. Cook for 45 mins over a low heat. 20 mins before the end of cooking boil the potatoes.

Sauté de veau à l'orange

Sauté of Veal with Orange

Take a piece of meat from the chump end. Cut it into pieces and brown in oil with onions. Add a small glass of white wine. Cover and cook over a low heat.

While it is cooking, zest two oranges and blanch them in boiling water, drain and rinse.

When the veal is cooked, remove it from the pan. Add salt and pepper. Throw away the fat and put the pan back on a hot flame, add a glass of white wine and leave to boil. Press the two oranges and add the juice to the pan. Stir and then pour over the veal.

Hunter's Rabbit

Navarin d'agneau aux petits légumes

Navarin of Lamb with Vegetables

Peel some pickling onions and turnips and quarter them if they are of average size or leave them whole if they are small. Slice the carrots, shell the peas (or use frozen peas which have been blanched, in this case add them 15 mins before the end of cooking). Peel the potatoes, quarter them and keep them in water.

Brown the pieces of shoulder of lamb and a little collar in oil. Add a tomato and a chopped onion. Add three glasses of water and leave to simmer. Then add all the vegetables, cover and cook over a very low heat.

Simmer for 40 mins and then uncover and leave to reduce a little. The potatoes will be added 20 mins before the navarin has finished cooking.

Tarte aux pommes anetaise

Anet Apple Tart

Roll out some puff pastry and peel and finely slice six russet apples. Butter a pie dish and lay out the pastry. Place the apple slices attractively around the dish with a rosace in the centre. Sprinkle with sugar. Beat an egg with half a glass of milk and pour over the tart. Bake for 45 mins.

Behind the door, Anet's flamboyant dining room. On this side of the door, a bright and modern kitchen, organised around a new Cornue kitchen range. On the table, the Anet Apple Tart.

GÂTEAU AU CHOCOLAT

Chocolate Cake

125g of butter,
a bar of dark chocolate (about 100g),
100g of sugar,
half a sachet of almond powder,
4 egg yolks and whites.

This cake must not be cooked completely and needs to be watched closely so that the inside remains creamy and runny when served.
Stiffen the egg whites and add the other ingredients and keep an eye on it while it is cooking.
Decorate with icing sugar and chocolate chips.

FLEURY-LA-FORÊT

Patienta et labore

Pierre and Kristina Caffin's guests take their breakfast in the kitchen surrounded by the 153 copper objects and the many items in earthenware. The castle has returned from a long absence after being almost completely abandoned for decades before being bought and restored by the Caffin family. The layout of this castle, built in the 13th century with brick and flint, is rectangular with four towers at each corner surrounded by the wings. In the Forêt de Lyons, famous for its old beech trees and its large stags, the heads of some of which are presented in the hall, the approach is majestic: a long alley of hundred-year old lime trees, then a long railing surrounding the ceremonial courtyard. Today refurnished, Fleury is also home to a collection of dolls which provide their own touch of fantasy in the selfless and long work involved in restoring a castle. The miniature kitchen, with its cast-iron stove, forms a pair with the real kitchen with its honeycomb-shaped floor slabs.

Top.
On the façade, the Courcoul coat-of-arms is still visible: an uprooted tree and the initials P.C. Pierre de Courcoul bought the fief of Fleury in 1559 and had the castle built but it was later destroyed by a fire in 1645. It was rebuilt as it is today and later extended with two wings.
Opposite.
The kitchen floor is remarkable, with hexagonal stone and clay slabs. This large room, still used today, saw the addition of a large cast-iron stove at the end of the 19th century to replace the fireplace.

Blanquette de veau façon Fleury

Fleury-Style Blanquette of Veal

Brown two onions and the veal. Add salt and pepper. When half-cooked, add the carrots and potatoes. Slow cook for 1 hour. Just before serving, add the cream and boil briefly.

Filet de cerf au calvados

Fillet of Stag with Calvados

A recipe which evokes the game-filled Forest of Lyons.

The day before, clean the fillet, soak it in Calvados and leave to macerate overnight. The next day, dry the fillet and brown it in a mixture of butter and oil in a thick-bottomed pan. Add salt and pepper and half a glass of Calvados. Heat and flambé. Remove the fillet and keep warm. Pour on 25cl of fresh cream, stir and bring to the boil for 2 mins. Add a heaped spoonful of warm apple jelly without boiling. Stir well. Cover the fillet with this sauce. Serve with a celery purée with apple or chestnuts.

Fleury-Style Blanquette of Veal.

The ceremonial courtyard.A solid and perfectly symmetrical castle.

Purée de céleri aux pommes

Celery Purée with Apples

Peel a large celery and cut it into pieces. Cover with water and cook for 20 mins. Add two large peeled and chopped apples. Cook for a further 10 mins. Liquidise and add 10cl of single cream and a large knob of butter.

Right.
After the Caumont family, it was a Lieutenant General of the King's army, Count Jacques Dauger, who bought the estate in 1768. On the plate of the kitchen's fireplace, the azure and gold coat-of-arms of his mother, Marie du Vidal, can be seen, as well as the motto «Patienta et labore».

Top.
Among the many copper kitchen objects, there are all sizes and shapes for frying, braising or boiling, as well as plates from a Montereau dinner service.

Opposite.
A charcoal filter from the end of the 19th century. It enabled the castle to be supplied with drinking water and offered the luxury of an indoor wash-house.

Purée de châtaignes

Chestnut Purée

Make an incision in 1kg of chestnuts. Boil them for 20 mins, drain and peel them. Place them in a pan with 1l of chicken stock and a bouquet garni. Cook for three-quarters of an hour over a low heat, drain them and blend them. Add about 30g of butter and two soup-spoons of fresh cream. Add salt and pepper to taste. If necessary, thin with a little cooking stock.

TARTE AUX FRAISES

Strawberry Tart

Shortcrust pastry: mix 150g of flour with 100g of sugar, add 60g of butter and form a ball. Set aside for 30 mins.

During this time, make a confectioner's custard with 100g of sugar, 60g of flour, four eggs and 50cl of milk which you pour hot over the preparation. Thicken.

Roll out the pastry and bake it. Spread the custard over the top and add the strawberries. Boil a little redcurrant jelly and spread it over the tart.

MANOIR DE VILLERS

Manor on the Seine

When leaving Rouen, the Seine flows through the meanders it has carved out with great patience. On its banks, there are many buildings, with fortified castles on the cliffs and abbeys on the plains. In one of the loops, the Manoir de Villers is as one with its refined park designed by a student of Achille Duchêne. This large Norman house, dating from the 16th century, was extended at the end of the 19th century in a charming Gothic Norman style, with a wing which opens out over the river where sometimes a cargo ship or a cruise boat passes by. The manor's course is in Caumont stone, the upper floors are timber-framed and the roof is covered with Normandy tiles. The same family has owned it for more than two hundred years and each beautiful object is in its rightful place. Here, the history of the silverware is a familiar story and it is known how to maintain a bowling-green and how to prepare an «ambigu». Monsieur and Madame Robert Méry de Bellegarde opened their door to us as well as their family notebooks and we discovered good family cuisine and also the fact that young turnips are delicious when eaten raw!

Top.
Pots-pourris in Dresden china. These vases are filled with sweet-smelling flowers and plants. They are remarkable for their meticulous floral decorations.
Opposite.
The castle's dining room opening out on to two facades. The stove is also a plate-warmer.

Behind the 18th century gate, a field belonging to the property offers the colours of an Impressionist painting on the banks of the Seine.

View from the Théâtre de Verdure, the manor's façade with the oldest part on the right and the 19th century wing on the left.

MENU of Wednesday 11 June

Fish mousse, green sauce
Salad, rib of chard, fennel, turnips
Chocolate Succulent
Caramel Eggs

MOUSSE DE POISSON

Fish Mousse

1kg of coalfish,
8 eggs,
1 large tin of tomato concentrate,
salt, pepper, tarragon.

Poach the coalfish in a court-bouillon but not for very long; mix the eggs and the tomato concentrate; salt, pepper and add the chopped tarragon. Add the fish broken into small pieces. Pour the mixture into a cake mould. Place in a bain-marie for 25 mins at Gas 5/6 and keep an eye on it.
Serve with a green sauce.

SAUCE VERTE

Green Sauce

Make a mayonnaise with peanut oil. Add a purée of tarragon, parsley, chives, spinach or only its juice. Another option is to use chervil and bronze fennel.

This table is a trompe l'œil which depicts the manor.

Among the many rare objects to be found, we chose this old knife and fork which dates from the time of Henry IV.

Œufs au caramel

Caramel Eggs

Heat 1l of milk with a vanilla pod split in half. Stiffen the egg whites until very firm. Poach spoonfuls of egg white in the simmering milk four at a time (the inside should not be cooked). Place them on a cloth. Keep the milk which will be used to make the custard along with eight egg yolks and four spoonfuls of sugar. Pour the creamy mixture into a bowl and add the egg whites. Make a caramel with a spoonful of water and ten sugar cubes. When it lightens, coat the eggs whites. Add flaked almonds if you wish.

This recipe is photographed on a Japanese-inspired table by Gallé.

Succulent au chocolat

Chocolate Succulent

250g of chocolate,
6 eggs,
250g of sugar,
250g of butter,
1/2 teaspoon of baking powder.

Melt the chocolate in a bain-marie with the butter. Add the sugar, the egg yolks and the flour. Stiffen the egg whites and add them to the mixture with care. Cook for 20 mins at Gas 6/7. Cook quickly so that the inside stays creamy.

Once cooked, cut the cake into rectangles and sprinkle with icing sugar.

Present on the family's Sevres service as here or on a service that you have at home.

Coffee is served in the «Jardin secret», on a Knights Templar table and on a service painted by Anne-Marie Méry de Bellegarde. The historic park has a wealth of secret corners and viewpoints, including two bowling greens surrounded by a hedge.

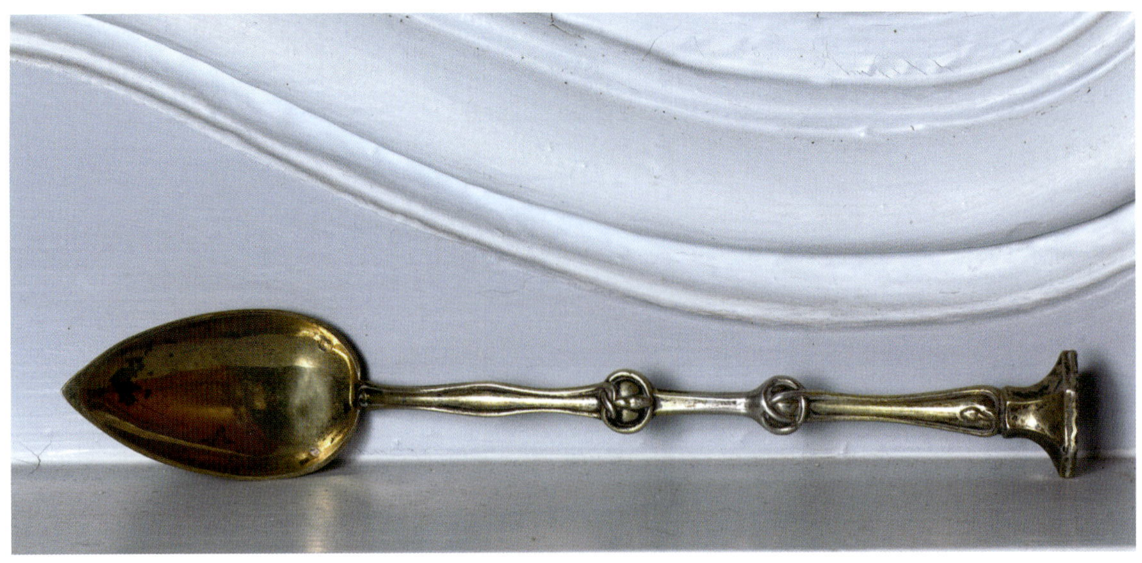

This old spoon was used to administer tablets after they had been crushed with the pestle at the other end.

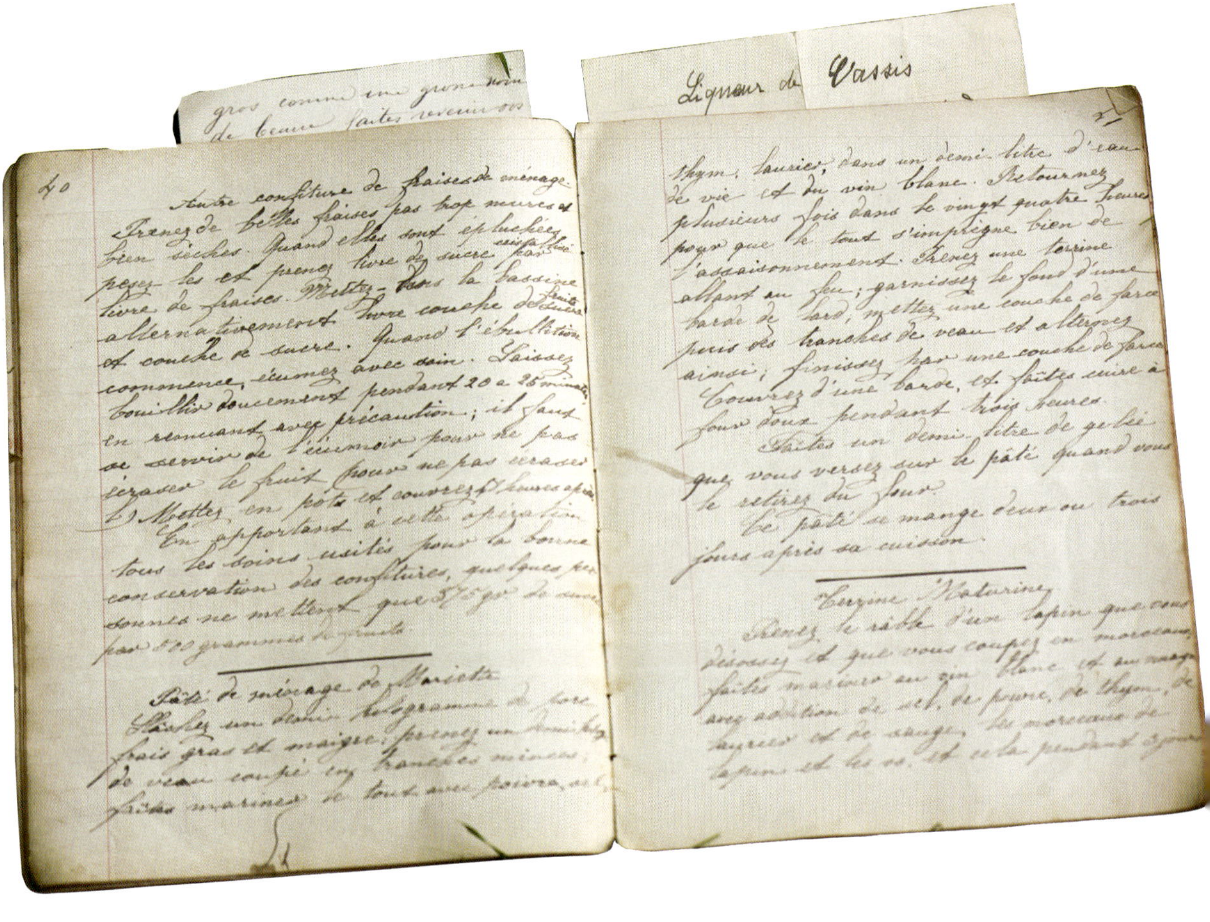

gros comme une grosse noix de beurre faites revenir ...

Liqueur de Cassis

40

Autre confiture de fraises de ménage

Prenez de belles fraises pas trop mûres et bien sèches. Quand elles sont épluchées pesez-les et prenez livre de sucre par livre de fraises. Mettez dans la bassine alternativement une couche de fruit et couche de sucre. Quand l'ébullition commence, écumez avec soin. Laissez bouillir doucement pendant 20 à 25 minutes en remuant avec précaution; il faut se servir de l'écumoir pour ne pas écraser le fruit. Mettez en pôts et couvrez [illegible]. En apportant à cette opération tous les soins usités pour la bonne conservation des confitures, quelques personnes ne mettent que 375 gr de sucre par 500 grammes de fruits.

Pâté de ménage de Mariette

Hachez un demi kilogramme de porc frais gras et maigre; prenez [illegible] tranches minces de veau coupé en [illegible] faites mariner le tout avec poivre, sel,

thym, laurier, dans un demi-litre d'eau de vie et du vin blanc. Retournez plusieurs fois dans les vingt quatre heures pour que le tout s'imprègne bien de l'assaisonnement. Prenez une terrine allant au feu; garnissez le fond d'une barde de lard, mettez une couche de farce puis des tranches de veau et alternez ainsi; finissez par une couche de farce. Couvrez d'une barde, et faites cuire à four doux pendant trois heures.

Faites un demi-litre de gelée que vous versez sur le pâté quand vous le retirez du four.

Ce pâté se mange deux ou trois jours après sa cuisson

Terrine Maturine

Prenez le râble d'un lapin que vous désossez et que vous coupez en morceaux faites macérer au vin blanc et au [illegible] avec addition de sel, de poivre, de thym, de laurier et de sauge, les morceaux de lapin et les os, et cela pendant [illegible]

Some extracts from the recipe book of Madame Delaporte, Madame Méry de Bellegarde's great-grandmother

RIS DE VEAU À L'OSEILLE

Calves' Sweetbreads with Sorrel

« Drain the calves' sweetbreads for one hour in cold water and blanch for 5 mins in salted water, rinse and remove the nerves. Steam for 40 mins. Deglaze with light gravy and serve with braised sorrel. »

NÈFLES AU BEURRE

Medlars with Butter

« Take some undamaged medlars and remove their stalks. Melt some butter in a pan and when it is white add the medlars with some caster sugar. Leave to boil, add a glass of Malaga. Reduce and serve warm. »

LIQUEUR DE CASSIS

Blackcurrant Liqueur

« Place 2kg of ripe seeded blackcurrants in narrow jars; add 300g of raspberries, 4l of 50 or 60° brandy. Seal well. Leave to infuse for two months (it is best to leave even longer). Decant and press the marc in order to remove all the juice and add 1kg of sugar. Sieve through a fine cloth and bottle. Blackcurrant improves greatly with age. »

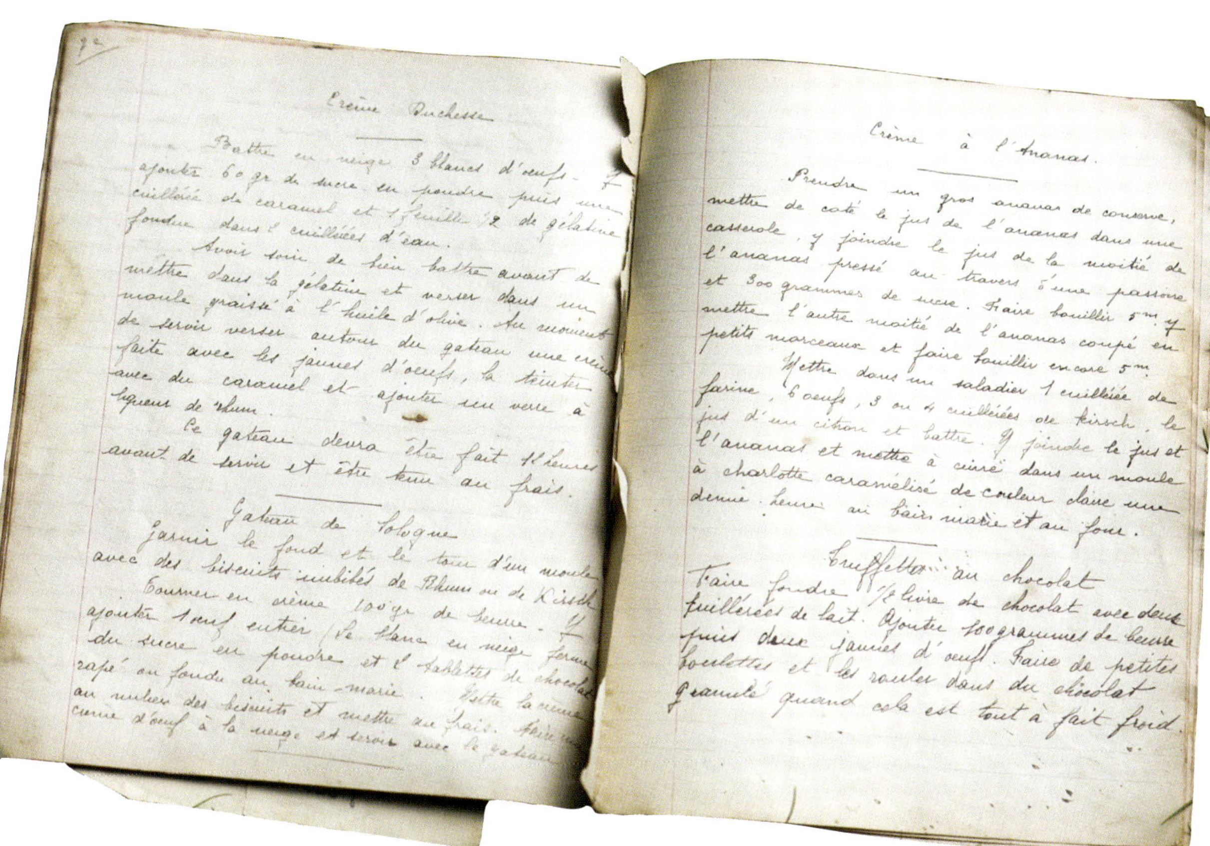

Crème Duchesse

Battre en neige 3 blancs d'oeufs. Y ajouter 60 gr de sucre en poudre puis une cuillerée de caramel et 1 feuille 1/2 de gélatine fondue dans 2 cuillerées d'eau.

Avoir soin de bien battre avant de mettre dans la gélatine et verser dans un moule graissé à l'huile d'olive. Au moment de servir verser autour du gateau une crème faite avec les jaunes d'oeufs, la teinter avec du caramel et ajouter un verre à liqueur de rhum.

Ce gateau devra être fait 12 heures avant de servir et être tenu au frais.

Gateau de Pologne

Garnir le fond et le tour d'un moule avec des biscuits imbibés de Rhum ou de Kirsch.

Tourner en crème 100 gr de beurre. Y ajouter 1 oeuf entier (le blanc en neige ferme) du sucre en poudre et 2 tablettes de chocolat rapé ou fondu au bain-marie. Mettre la crème au milieu des biscuits et mettre au frais. Faire une crème d'oeuf à la neige et servir avec le gateau.

Crème à l'Ananas.

Prendre un gros ananas de conserve, mettre de coté le jus de l'ananas dans une casserole, y joindre le jus de la moitié de l'ananas pressé au travers d'une passoire et 300 grammes de sucre. Faire bouillir 5m. Y mettre l'autre moitié de l'ananas coupé en petits morceaux et faire bouillir encore 5m.

Mettre dans un saladier 1 cuillerée de farine, 6 oeufs, 3 ou 4 cuillerées de kirsch, le jus d'un citron et battre. Y joindre le jus et l'ananas et mettre à cuire dans un moule à charlotte caramélisé de couleur claire une demie heure au bain marie et au four.

Truffettes au chocolat

Faire fondre 1/2 livre de chocolat avec deux cuillerées de lait. Ajouter 100 grammes de beurre puis deux jaunes d'oeuf. Faire de petites boulettes et les rouler dans du chocolat granulé quand cela est tout à fait froid.

FILIÈRES

The spice road

Everything at Filières invites you to distant shores: the Persan weapons, «d'azur a trois demoiselles (which are butterflies) volant en bande», the wallpaper in the Chinese salon or the branches of tea from Africa. In the Pays de Caux, where the chalk cliffs fall into the sea which they tint with a cream-coloured cloud, the Château de Filières is devoted to spices which, along with ivory, made the fortune of the ports of Dieppe and Fécamp. Spices were gifts for Kings, a currency of exchange, sometimes even spoils of war. In these ports of precious silk and china, which can still be admired at Filières, tea was drunk and eaten in all its forms.

Originally, there was a fortress, of which, in dry weather, it is still possible to see the marks in the middle of the courtyard. Then a Henry IV castle which Alexandre-Charles de Catteville, Marquis of Mirville, decided to replace with a majestic classical castle, the plans of which are attributed to Victor Louis. Work started in 1785, but the shrewd Marquis only destroyed the old castle progressively. The replacement building was stopped at the Revolution, giving Filières the composite character which it has maintained since, set inside its dried moats and within a large *clos-masure*, a enclosure of tall beech trees which is so typical of the Pays de Caux.

The Château de Filières has always been passed down the family through inheritance, from Hocquart de Turtoy to Bonguy, the Marquis de Persan who, along with his wife, looks after the series of salons which open out on to distant shores.

This is the most striking room in Filières: the Chinese salon.
These wallpaper paintings were imported from the Far East two centuries ago.

Menu of 24 Octobre

Broth
Smoked Salmon
Cheese from Lille
Filières Delights

Bouillon

Broth

Take a small piece of chuck steak and half a chicken and chop roughly. Put this meat in a cooking pot with a chopped leek, a sliced carrot, a stick of celery, and a chopped onion. Cover with 3l of water. Bring to the boil stirring from time to time.

Turn down the heat and simmer for 30 mins and add a few cloves, some parsely, coarse salt and pepper.

Then blend the broth, remove the fat and add a few dashes of caramel to give it colour.

Top.
Here are two splendid «Imari», huge tea fountains of brought back from Japan in the 18th century.

Bottom.
Filières Delights.

Délices de Filières

Filières Delights

Prepare some tea (at Filières, every hour and every use for tea, this one is called N° 243).

Stone some prunes and put them in the simmering tea. Add some orange and lemon peel, some cinnamon, ginger, etc. Leave to macerate in the fridge. This dessert will be served in an attractive fruit bowl and will be eaten with vanilla ice-cream or Grand Marnier.

Dinner service bearing the Hocquart de Turtot coat-of-arms. Persan cutlery. The piers are decorated with 18th century style antique medallions. Vieux Rouen wall lamps, Canton vases, a samovar, a steamer for cooking boiled eggs… history and exoticism combine in the magical atmosphere of the dining room at Filières.

GÂTEAU DE LA REINE

Queen's Cake

Three large bars of chocolate, 125g of butter, 125g of caster sugar, 60g of vanilla sugar, 3 eggs, 50g of almond powder, 2 soup-spoons of flour.

Melt the butter, add the chocolate and leave to melt slowly. Add the caster sugar, vanilla sugar and almond powder. When everything has melted, mix the chocolate with the flour and egg yolks on the side of the stove. Butter a mould and stiffen the egg whites and add to the mixture. Pour into the mould and cook in a hot oven for 40 mins. This cake is served with custard.

Filières is as rural as it is mannered. Rural through its location and the use made of its buildings. Mannered through the layout of its salons and its collections from foreign shores.

Boudin de Saint-Rémy-de-Colbosc

Saint-Rémy-de-Colbosc Pudding

This is a neighbouring village to Filières. This old local speciality contains farm-style cream and Calvados in pork tripe skin with a large piece of fat bacon at the centre.

Prick the puddings before cooking. Brush with a little oil. Place them in the oven. Lay out one apple for each pudding. Core the apple and put in a small piece of butter and a little cinnamon. Cook in a hot oven keeping an eye on them. Serve with mashed potatoes.

Saint-Rémy-de-Colbosc Pudding.

Scones

Sixteen soup-spoons of flour, one teaspoon of salt, one soup-spoon of baking powder. Mix it all together and add a soup-spoon of butter. Rub together and add enough milk to form a soft dough (about one cup of milk). Knead the dough as little as possible. Press out the dough on a board to a thickness of 1cm with your hand and use an egg cup to cut out the scones. Sprinkle the baking tin with flour and bake in a hot oven for 15 to 20 mins. Do not let them brown too much and do not turn them over.
Cut them in half, butter them and serve hot.

Scones in front of a rare silver tea service.

Biscuits au thé

Tea Biscuits

For 250g of flour, take 125g of unsalted butter, 80g of brown sugar and a little water. Infuse one teaspoon of tea leaves in very little water, strain them and set aside the tea; add the small wet tea leaves to the flour and mix with the other ingredients along with the tea. Do not add too much tea at a time or the dough will be too wet. Leave for half an hour.
Preheat the oven at 200 °C.
Roll out the pastry very thinly. Cut out small biscuits and lay them on a baking tray.
Bake for 10 minutes keeping a close eye on them.

Mousse au chocolat

Chocolate Mousse

The day before making this dessert, marinate 250g of raisins in cognac or another spirit.
Take two bars of dark chocolate and break it into pieces and melt in a spoonful of water or in a bain-marie. Remove from the heat and add 50g of butter, four spoonfuls of cold cream and four egg yolks. Stiffen the egg whites. Mix everything together with a spatula. Add the well-drained raisins and a teaspoon of coffee essence.

Fromage blanc aux épices

Fromage Frais with Spices

Mix some fat-free fromage frais with the equivalent of half its weight of fat-free yoghurt.
Infuse a pinch of saffron in two soup-spoons of hot skimmed milk; sieve the milk and add the fromage frais and yoghurt mixture. Add a pinch of nutmeg, some cardamom and two cinnamon sticks.
Sugar is not necessary because the spices replace it.

CANY

The Grand Siècle in the Pays de Caux

A beautiful example of the Louis XIII style in the Pays de Caux, the Château de Cany stands on a small island in the Durdent Valley, three leagues from the sea. Built by Pierre Le Marinier, the Lord of Cany, in 1682, it was sold to Becdelièvre and has never been sold since, passing to Montmorency-Luxembourg, then to the Barons of Hunolstein – the reason for the initials M.L.H. on the crockery and the kitchen utensils – and finally to the Dreux-Brézé family. The castle is of exemplary legibility: outside, a monumental forecourt, surrounded by outbuildings, which extends towards the gardens, ornamental ponds and moats, beautiful railings and a park redesigned in an English style in the 19th century. Inside, particular care has been taken with the layout of the rooms: each wing has a staircase and the series of large salons open out on to both facades. The castle has preserved its precious original furniture, beautiful paintings, libraries and archives and family souvenirs. The recipes passed on to us by Countess Antoine de Dreux-Brézé, born Gilone d'Harcourt – an important family in Normandy – are those of the Pays de Caux: herring and mackerel from Fécamp, Yvetot chicken and the famous Canard à la Presse.

The signs of Mansart's hand can be seen in this beautiful castle surrounded by water.

Poulet d'Yvetot aux pommes

Yvetot Chicken with Apples

Yvetot is the most famous «franc-alleu» in France. A small territory in the Pays de Caux enjoying all the privileges of the sovereignty until the 16th century (Henri IV, a great enthusiast of poultry if ever there was one, said: «If I lose the Kingdom of France, I will always have Yvetot!»), transmitted as a principality, Yvetot was overturned in the Revolution. Today, there is no more King of Yvetot, although a title of Prince existed up to this century.

This recipe is simple provided that the chicken is good. Brown well on both sides and cook in a cocotte. When it is ready, add salt and pepper and remove it from its dish; set it aside somewhere warm. Throw away the fat and deglaze with Calvados and flambé it. Add a little butter and fine slices of russet or boskoop apples. When they are cooked, lay them around the chicken which the maître d'hôtel will carve on the occasional table.

Canard de Duclair

Duclair Duck

Duclair ducks, bred on the banks of the Seine, are black with a white breast.

Here is a local recipe: the duck will be roasted on the spit for about fifteen minutes because it should be rosy but have lost its fat. Remove the wings and drumsticks, salt and pepper them and coat them with strong mustard. Place the wings and drumsticks under the grill for about 5 mins. Then, remove the skin and cut relatively thin fillets of breast. Coat with the sauce prepared earlier which can be kept in the fridge for several days.

The sauce is prepared as follows: chop 1kg of onions and brown them in butter over a low heat. When they are well browned, but not burnt, add a bottle of red wine, Bordeaux for example, and simmer gently for 3 hours. When it has reduced, bind with butter, put in a jar and keep in the fridge.

Before serving, heat gently and pour over the duck.

Did you know that turkey is called «picot», meaning Jesuit or priest, in the Pays de Caux? It is fed from its youngest age with a mixture of herbs, nettle leaves and egg yolks to fortify it. «Guzzling some priest» was a popular expression during turkey festivals... although, maybe it was not that much of a festival for the turkeys themselves!

Yvetot Chicken with Apples. The sauceboat with an attractive peacock's tail bears the initials C.A.N.Y.

Safattes aux haricots blancs

Safattes with White Beans

These are herring split in two and placed in brine and then smoked with beech chips.
Grill them on the embers for a few minutes in September or October. Serve them with white beans or Soissons beans and a creamy pepper sauce without salt, which has been thickened with an egg yolk.

Maquereaux

Mackerel

Remove the heads, empty them and cut them along the back following the backbone; roughly grind a large quantity of pepper and rub into the skin. Dry them in the sun for two or three days fastened by the tail. Remove any excess pepper. Cook in the oven or under the grill and serve as they are with some lemon or a drop of warm cream.

A thick table, a sturdy stove: the kitchen in Cany is well equipped to serve a large house.

These unusual - and rare - kitchen spoons with the initials M.L.H. could be used for two purposes.

57
40 K 57-18

MIROMESNIL

In a nourishing garden

In the heart of its woods and its beech trees «which fight all year against the sea and the wind», according to the words of Maupassant, the Château de Miromesnil is surrounded by greenery, even the tennis court is a lawn. The walls are covered with all sorts of clematis and the trees in its vegetable garden form a pair with the garlands of flowers on its beautiful façade. The garden is as ornamental as it is utilitarian: its flowers decorate the castle's salons, its vegetables provide food for the table and its fruit perfumes the kitchen.

An initial fortified castle was destroyed in 1589 during Henry IV's fight for the throne. The Dyel de Miromesnil family replaced it with a beautiful building in Varengville brick and Caen stone. The façade overlooking the courtyard is in a Louis XIII monumental style: the brick walls are covered with decorations of pilasters and grotesque masks surmounted by urns placed at the base of the roof which was highlighted by the addition of two wings in the 19th century.

Miromesnil was untouched during the Revolution: Armand Thomas Hue de Miromesnil, the Minister of Justice under Louis XVI, wrote a royal act in 1780, abolishing the «*question*», a torture inflicted on prisoners to make them confess, which earned him the protection of the population. The castle then passed to the Corday d'Aubigny family, then to the Marescot family. We were received by Count and Countess Thierry de Vogüé for a gourmet day around many gourmet products. Miromesnil now belongs to their niece, Nathalie Romatet.

The private kitchen in the Château de Miromesnil all in green. The ceiling is a brick vault. With its attractive Cornue kitchen range the room is organised around the work surfaces. At the back, the fruit bowl holds the apples and pears picked in the orchard.

Less exuberant than the northern façade, the southern façade is in a pure Henry IV style. Varengeville brick combines with Caen stone at the end of a perspective filled with greenery and large trees.

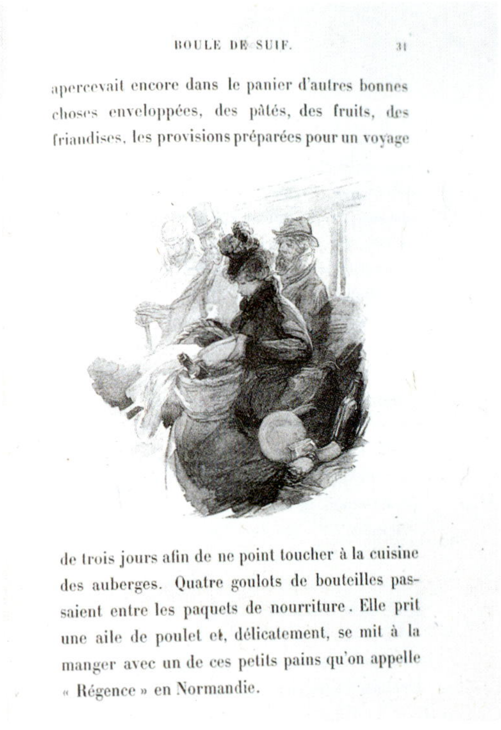

BOULE DE SUIF. 31

apercevait encore dans le panier d'autres bonnes choses enveloppées, des pâtés, des fruits, des friandises, les provisions préparées pour un voyage

de trois jours afin de ne point toucher à la cuisine des auberges. Quatre goulots de bouteilles passaient entre les paquets de nourriture. Elle prit une aile de poulet et, délicatement, se mit à la manger avec un de ces petits pains qu'on appelle « Régence » en Normandie.

On 5 August 1850, while the castle was rented to the Maupassant family, the writer who, for all time, will be the best ever storyteller of Norman passions, was born: Guy de Maupassant. Although he did not live there for very long, he often wrote about the Pays de Caux. The novel «Boule de Suif» which castigated with realism men and women's mediocrity, is set in Tôtes, not very far from Miromesnil. The original edition is presented in the castle's hall along with other souvenirs of the writer. Despite his short time in Miromesnil, it is possible to find the ambience of the Pays de Caux in Maupassant's stories - the large farmyards which are home to crafty farmers and the long and, windy winters.
Maupassant's life was very tragic: ten years of prolific writing, then illness, madness and death.
His writing is limpid… as calm as water.

Extract from the Terrier de Miromesnil

«Louis Gilles, a bourgeois from Dieppe, owns the inheritance and plots of land in the parish of Saint-Aubin-sur-Scie outlined below:

- the first plot of *masure* with closely built houses and buildings is planted (...), for which is due to the lord, the seigniorial rent each year of 5 sols, 6 deniers and 4 capons at Saint-Michel, 4 deniers at Christmas and 20 eggs 2 deniers at Easter;
- the second plot for tilling (...), the third plot for tilling...
- the total amount due is one quart of barley, one quart of oats, 52 eggs, 6 capons.»

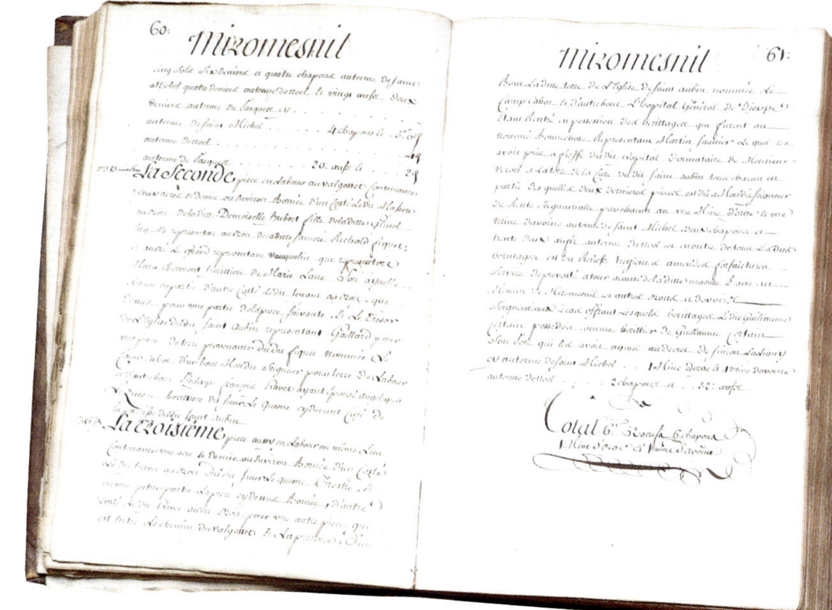

60 Miromesnil

La Seconde

La Troisième

Miromesnil 61

Note: the *clos-masure* in the Pays de Caux is a farm popularised in the novels of Maupassant. Surrounded by trees, often several rows of them, the farm buildings formed an enclosure which the «*horsain*», foreigner, entered very rarely.

Madame de Vogüé's enclosed vegetable garden was famous. Thierry de Vogüé has continued maintaining it in order to supply the house with food for sustenance and for the pleasure of visitors. In the autumn, the garden of Miromesnil rests, but not the gardeners: there is always work to be done for a bright spring and a radiant summer.

*M*ENU of 4 November

Shortbread Biscuits with Cheddar
Miromesnil Griddle Cakes
Chicken Pie
Conversation
Romanée Saint-Vivant 1958

SABLÉS AU CHEDDAR OU À LA MIMOLETTE

Shortbread Biscuits with Cheddar or Mimolette Cheese

For an aperitif. They will keep for a long time in a tin box.

200g of flour
80g of butter,
100g of cheddar, or semi-steamed Mimolette,
paprika, salt and pepper.

Grate the cheese. Soften the butter. Mix all the ingredients together to obtain a pastry. Roll it out and cut out small biscuit shapes. Lay them on a buttered oven tray. Bake in a preheated oven at a medium temperature.

GALETTE DE MIROMESNIL

Miromesnil Cakes

For 8 people

Make a white sauce with 30g of butter, 60g of flour, 50cl of milk, 4 egg yolks, 500g of cream and 500g of Parmesan. When the white sauce is ready, leave to cool. Stiffen the egg whites. Add them to the white sauce.

Butter sixteen small cylindrical cake moulds (see photo) and pour in the mixture. Bake in a medium oven (preheated) in a bain-marie. Take them out of the oven once they have risen well; do not exceed 25 mins in the oven. Butter a gratin dish. Remove the cakes from the moulds, cover them with a little single cream and season with nutmeg.

Before serving, put the cakes in a medium oven so that they are hot and well-risen.

The Shortbread Biscuits with Cheddar may be cut into amusing shapes. The Miromesnil Cakes are like small soufflés when baked in the oven a second time.

Chicken Pie.

Pie de poulet

Chicken Pie

Take a large farm-style chicken, eight slices of bacon, 400g of parasol mushrooms, 5 shallots, parsley, thyme, salt and pepper. Puff pastry: 300g of flour, 150g of butter, salt, pepper and a glass of Champagne. Carve the chicken. Brown all the pieces in a high-sided frying pan with very little butter until they are lightly browned. Remove any excess fat with kitchen roll. Butter an oven dish and lay the bacon slices on the bottom and the sides and add the chicken pieces. Add the cleaned and uncooked parasol mushrooms, chopped shallots, parsley and thyme. Add the glass of Champagne. Cover with the puff pastry, wetting the sides of the dish before applying the ends of the pastry. Glaze the top with egg yolk. Decorate the top with a sharp knife. Bake in a medium oven for about 30 mins until the pastry is golden brown.

Conversation

300g of puff pastry,
vanilla confectioner's custard
comprising: 50cl of milk,
6 egg yolks, 50g of flour,
80g of caster sugar,
125g of powdered almonds.

Prepare the pie dish with the puff pastry, pour in the confectioner's custard preparation and the almonds. Cover with the other half of puff pastry. Coat the top with royal icing comprising half an egg white to which icing sugar has been added and whipped until thick. Decorate with four strips of pastry to create diamond shapes which, too, are coated with royal icing. Bake in a hot oven for 30 mins. The Conversation is eaten cold.

This dessert dates from the end of the 18th century and it is said that it takes its name from a book by Madame d'Epingy called «Les Conversations d'Emilie».

Ramequins au fromage ou Choux au fromage

Cheese Ramekins or Cheese Choux

Prepare a choux pastry for 6 people: put 50cl of water, 125g of butter and a pinch of fine salt into a saucepan and heat. Once the butter has melted, add the 250g of sieved flour in one go and stir with a wooden spoon; leave on the heat and dry out the mixture stirring until it comes unstuck from the saucepan. Remove from the heat and add an egg and stir well. When it has been absorbed, add a second egg and continue until the eighth egg.

Bake twelve oval-shaped choux which have been piped on to a baking try in a medium oven. Leave to cool. Cut the top off the choux and add the following preparation: make a roux with 140g of butter and 140g of flour. Add 1l of warm milk and stir until thick, then add 500g of parmesan and stir. Fill each choux and put back in the oven before serving.

Mozzarella in carrozza

Recipe from Madame de Vogüé who is of Italian descent. Made in the same way as French Toast.

Take two slices of dried bread, soak them in milk and dip in flour, and place a slice of mozzarella between them. Seal the edges with egg yolk. Heat a little olive oil in a frying pan and when it is very hot, brown them on each side. Place them on some kitchen roll. Pepper copiously and make the shape of a cross with anchovies.

Tajine

Take 1kg of mutton (which has more taste than lamb). Brown three onions (chopped in olive oil) in the tajine over a very low heat with the mutton cut into pieces. Add pepper, salt, ginger and saffron (a pinch if it is real saffron).

Soak with a few glasses of water and add various vegetables (turnips, carrots, courgettes, etc) and a teaspoon of tomato concentrate for colour. Cover and leave over a gentle heat for about 1 hour. One quarter of an hour before the end, add potatoes cut into quarters and blanched green olives.

Left page.
The dining room.
The Louis XVI woodwork, introduced in 1860, is decorated with pelicans and fish, both religious symbols.
The silverware bears the coat-of-arms of Albert de Mun, Thierry de Vogüé's great-grandfather, a politician of social Catholicism.

Glace de viande

Meat Ice-Cream

Brown some beef and veal bones with onions (never mutton) and brown 1kg of knuckle of beef in oil. Add some onions, carrots, a bouquet garni and a piece of pork rind. Cover with water, add salt, pepper and «four spices». Boil lightly on the corner of the stove for three days and three nights without interruption. Add the bones and any remains of chicken but never use duck or mutton; skim when necessary. Add more water from time to time, except on the last day, and leave to reduce. Remove the bones and sieve them. Leave to reduce over a low heat until you have obtained a thick, dark gravy, similar to a paste once it has cooled. Place in the fridge.

This meat ice-cream, now very rare, is used in very small doses for an excellent basis for sauces worthy of the great recipes of former times. Unfortunately, freeze-drying has replaced this culinary essential.

The office holds many books bound with the coat-of-arms of Hue de Miromesnil, three boar heads, here surmounted by a judge's cap.

Bottom.
A heart-shaped ice-cream maker.

Alphabetical INDEX

A dream 96
Anet Apple Tart 102
Apple Aspic 47
Apple Charlotte 32
Apple & Pear Crumble 20
Apple Royal 56
Apple Terrine with Gingerbread 90
Aristocrats 96

Balleroy Allumettes 28
Bathroom Pudding 81
Beef Tournedos with Colonel's Cream 71
Beef with Carrots 20
Blackcurrant Liqueur 117
Bon Jeune Homme 48
Bourdots 35
Bovary-Style Chitterlings Sausage 35
Braised Veal Joint 32
Broth 120
Buckwheat Mixture 10

Cabbage stuffed with Chestnuts 94
Caen-Style Shortbread Biscuits 35
Caen-Style Sole Matelote 44
Caen-Style Tripe 34
Calves' Sweetbreads with Sorrel 117
Canard à la Presse 126
Can't-Go-Wrong Apple Jelly 65
Caramel Eggs 114
Carrot Cake 97
Celery Purée with Apples 107
Charlotte with Almonds 40
Chartreuse of Pheasant or Partridge 96
Cheese Ramekins or Cheese Choux 136
Cheese Soufflé 20
Chestnut Cake 23
Chestnut Purée 108
Chicken Liver Paté 22
Chicken Pie 135
Chicken with Camembert 38
Chicken with Cider 8
Chicken with White Wine 61
Chicons with Shrimps 33
Chocolate Cake 103
Chocolate Mousse 123
Chocolate Royal 55
Chocolate Succulent 114
Chopped Chicons Salad with Roquefort and Walnuts 33
Cinzano Aperitif 52
Cod in Aspic 22
Colombières-Style Duck 23
Conserving Strawberry Juice 49
Conversation 135

Duclair Duck 128
Duo of Sea Bass and Matignon of Vegetables with a Virgin Sauce 15

Eggs Cooked in Milk 11
English Shortbread 39

Farm-Style Terrine 62
Feathered Game 76
Filières Delights 120
Fillet of Stag with Calvados 106
Fire-Grilled Chops of Wild Boar 89
Fish Mousse 113
Fleury-Style Blanquette of Veal 106
Fricandeau with Vendeuvre Sauce 52
Fromage Frais with Spices 123

Glazed Petits Fours 57
Green Sauce 113
Grenadine of Veal with Sorrel 80
Guinea Fowl with Raisins 79

Hard-Boiled Egg Croquettes 80
Hare à la Royale 52
Hunter's Rabbit 102

Ile d'Amour 61
Iron-baked Rice Pudding 8

Kidneys Belle Gourmande 53

La Petite Oie 84
Lard Soup 10

Le Veneur Venison Chops 88
Leek and Salmon Tart 22
Leg of Venison 76
Livarot and Pont l'Évêque Pie 73
Lobster with Garden Herbs and Coral 26

Mackerel 129
Madame Eloffe's Tuna Bread 40
Malakoff 40
Marie-Victoire Shortbread Biscuit with Red Fruit and Wine Jelly 16
Marquis 99
Meat Ice-Cream 137
Medlars with Butter 117
Miromesnil Cakes 134
Mozzarella in Carrozza 137
Mrs Forbes' Chocolate Cream 28

Navarin of Lamb with Vegetables 102
Norman Diplomate with Calvados 56
Normandy-Style Diablotins 55
Normandy Sole 61

Œufs Victoire 22
Oilliamson Sauce 32
Orange Pound Cake 99

Pears à la Bonne Femme 63
Pheasant with Chicons 33
Pike with Sancerre Cream 53
Potatoes 54
Prawn Vol-au-Vents 61
Pumpkin and Apple Jam 65

Queen's Cake 121

Rabbit Paté 52
Rabbit with Mustard 39
Republicans 96
Rhubarb Pie 79
Roast Pork with Apricots 23

Safattes with White Beans 129
Saint Peter's Cake 99
Saint-Rémy-de-Colbosc Pudding 122
Salmis of Pigeon with Pommeau 72
Sandwich Claude 52
Sang-Chaud 10

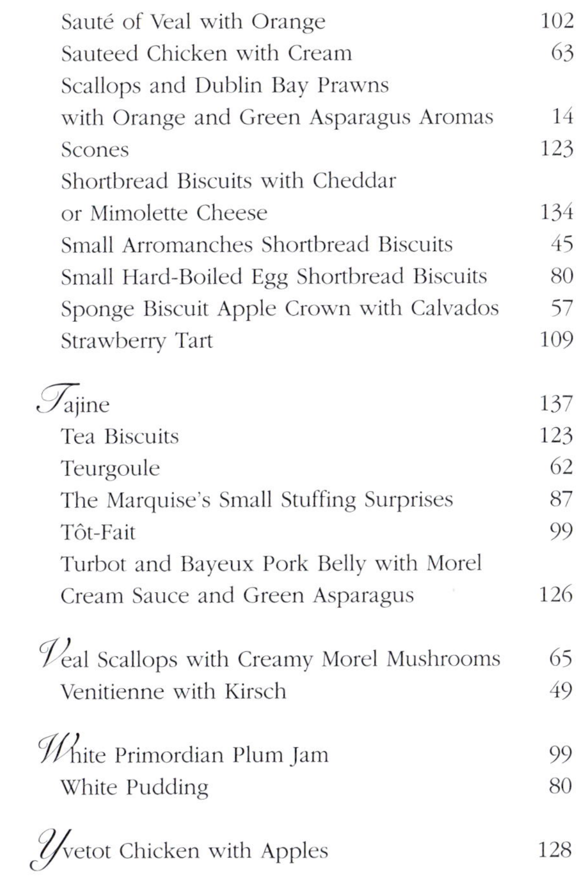

Sauté of Veal with Orange 102
Sauteed Chicken with Cream 63
Scallops and Dublin Bay Prawns with Orange and Green Asparagus Aromas 14
Scones 123
Shortbread Biscuits with Cheddar or Mimolette Cheese 134
Small Arromanches Shortbread Biscuits 45
Small Hard-Boiled Egg Shortbread Biscuits 80
Sponge Biscuit Apple Crown with Calvados 57
Strawberry Tart 109

Tajine 137
Tea Biscuits 123
Teurgoule 62
The Marquise's Small Stuffing Surprises 87
Tôt-Fait 99
Turbot and Bayeux Pork Belly with Morel Cream Sauce and Green Asparagus 126

Veal Scallops with Creamy Morel Mushrooms 65
Venitienne with Kirsch 49

White Primordian Plum Jam 99
White Pudding 80

Yvetot Chicken with Apples 128

The report is finished. It is safe for the chickens to come out again!

Practical GUIDE

Château de Crosville
50360 Crosville-sur-Douve
Listed Historic Monument. Member of VMF and DH.
Visits every afternoon from Easter to the end of September. Thematic exhibitions, shows. Norman evenings. Plant Days in April.
Owner: Mme Lefol.
Telephone: 02 33 41 67 25
Website: www.chateaucrosville.com

Château de Canisy
50750 Canisy
Listed Historic Monument. Member of VMF and DH.
Meetings, seminars.
Owners: M and Mme Denis de Kergorlay.
Telephone: 02 33 56 61 06
Fax: 02 33 55 92 75
Website: www.canisy.com

Château de Colombières
14710 Colombières
Listed Historic Monument. Member of VMF and DH.
Visits in July and August, except weekends. Weekends in September. Group visits from May to October on prior reservation. Light Festival (information at Bayeux and Isigny Tourist Offices). Bed & Breakfast, member of «Châteaux Accueil» and «Bienvenue au Château».
Owners: M and Mme Charles de Maupeou d'Ableiges.
Telephone: 02 31 22 51 65
Fax: 02 31 92 24 92
Website: www.chateaudecolombieres.com

Château de Balleroy
14490 Balleroy
Listed Historic Monument. Member of VMF and DH.
Castle, Balloon Museum and park open to the public from 15 March to 30 June and from 1 September to 15 October every day, except Tuesdays, from 10am to 12pm and from 2pm to 6pm. From July to August, every day from 10am to 6pm. Possible for groups to have lunch at the castle from Monday to Friday on prior reservation.
Owner: Forbes Family.
Telephone: 02 31 21 60 61
Fax: 02 31 21 51 77
Website: www.chateau-balleroy.com

Château de Fontaine-Henry
14160 Thaon
Listed Historic Monument. Member of VMF and DH.
Visits at weekends from Easter to All-Saints and every day, except Tuesdays, from 15 June to 15 September. International park of monumental sculptures.
Owner: Oilliamson Family.
Telephone: 06 89 84 85 57
Fax: 02 31 08 17 00
Website: www.chateau-de-fontaine-henry.com

Château de Fontaine-Etoupefour
14790 Fontaine-Etoupefour
Listed Historic Monument. Member of VMF and DH.
Visits of the exteriors, Mondays to Wednesdays, from July to September.
Owner: M. du Laz.
Telephone: 02 31 26 73 20

Château de Canon
14270 Mézidon-Canon
Listed Historic Monument. Member of VMF and DH.
Visits to the park and gardens every day from 1 June to 30 September, 2pm to 6pm. Weekends and public holidays from 10 April to 30 September.
Owner: Mézerac Family.
Telephone: 02 31 20 71 50 – 06 15 41 85 90
Website: www.chateaucanon.com

Château de Vendeuvre
14170 Vendeuvre
Listed Historic Monument. Member of VMF.
Visits from 1 April to 30 September every day from 11am to 6pm. October: Sundays and public holidays and school holidays. Tulip Festival in April, castle, park, «surprise» water garden, exotic garden, museum of miniature furniture. Restaurant for groups.
Owners: M et Mme de Vendeuvre.
Telephone: 02 31 40 93 83
Fax: 02 31 40 11 11
Website: www.vendeuvre.com

Manoir de Champ-Versant
14340 Bonnebosq
ISMH.
Guided tours exteriors by appointment all year, individuals and groups. Bed & breakfast, gite.

Owners: M et Mme Letrésor.
Telephone: 02 31 65 11 07
Fax: 02 31 65 11 07

Manoir de Saint-Hippolyte
14100 Saint-Martin-de-la-Lieue
Listed Historic Monument.
Unaccompanied and guided visits all year: discovery of the Saint-Hippolyte estate: historic, rural, agricultural heritage; riches of the Norman region – farm, Norman breeds of dairy cows, operational cheese factory – hire of rooms and catering, workshops.
Owner: Genois.
Telephone: 02 31 31 30 68
Fax: 02 31 31 83 72
Contact: genois@wanadoo.fr
Website: www.sitesremarquablesdugout.com

Château de Sassy
61750 Saint-Christophe-le-Jajolet
Listed Historic Monument. Member of VMF and DH.
Visits at weekends from Palm Sunday to 15 June. Every day from 15 June to 15 September.
Owner: Mme d'Audiffret-Pasquier.
Telephone: 02 33 35 32 66 – 02 33 35 36 90
Contact chateaudesassy@orange.fr

Château de Carrouges
61320 Carrouges
Listed Historic Monument.
Managed by the Centre for Historic Monuments. Visits to the castle and park every day except on 1 January, 1 May, 1 and 11 November, 25 December. Group visits on prior reservation. Cultural season, private and professional receptions, personalised reception.
Owner: the State.
Administrator: Mme Claude-Catherine Terrier.
Telephone: 02 33 31 16 42
Contact chateau.carrouges@monuments-nationaux.fr
Website: www.monuments-nationaux.fr

Château de Bonneville
27270 Le Chamblac
Listed ISMH. Member of VMF and DH.
Visits to listed gardens from May to September.
Owner:: Mme Charles-Edouard de Broglie.
Telephone: 02 32 44 63 56

Château d'Anet
28260 Anet
Listed Historic Monument. Member of VMF and DH.
Visits from 1 April to 3 October every day except Tuesdays. Group visits on prior reservation.
Owners: M and Mme de Yturbe.
Telephone: 02 37 41 90 07
Fax: 02 37 41 96 45
Website: www.chateaudanet.com

Château de Fleury-la-Forêt
27480 Fleury-la-Forêt
Listed Historic Monument. Member of DH.
Visits from 15 March to 15 October on Sundays and public holidays. In July and August, every day from 2pm to 6pm. Bed & breakfast in the castle.
Owners: M and Mme Caffin.
Telephone: 02 32 49 63 91
Website: www.chateau-fleury-la-foret.com

Manoir de Villers
76113 Saint-Pierre-de-Manneville
Listed ISMH. Member of VMF and DH.
Visits from April to October on weekends and public holidays. Two bed & breakfasts, one of which is a suite.
Owners: M and Mme Méry de Bellegarde.
Telephone/Fax: 02 35 32 07 02
Website: www.chateau-fleury-la-foret.com

Château de Filières
76430 Gommerville
Listed ISMH. Member of DH.
Visits in May and June on Sundays and public holidays. In July and August, every day from 11am to 6pm and on Heritage Days.
Owners: M and Mme de Persan.
Telephone: 02 35 20 53 30

Château de Cany
76540 Cany-Barville
Listed Historic Monument. Member of DH.
Visits in July and August.
Owners: M and Mme Antoine de Dreux-Brézé.
Telephone: 02 35 97 70 32

Château de Miromesnil
76550 Tourville-sur-Arques
Listed ISMH. Member of VMF and DH.
Visits from 1 April to 1 November from 2pm to 6pm; in addition to usual times, in July and August, from 10am to 1pm, unaccompanied visit to the gardens. Bed & breakfast, cooking lessons.
Owners: M and Mme Romatet.
Telephone: 02 35 85 02 80
Fax: 02 35 85 55 05
Website: www.chateaumiromesnil.com

Abbreviations: MH: Historic Monument. *ISMH:* Inventaire Supplémentaire des Monuments Historiques. *VMF:* association des Vieilles Maisons Francaises. *DH:* association la Demeure Historique.

CARTE ROUTIÈRE
DE
NORMANDIE.
CHERBOURG
Beaumont
Cap la Hougue
Barfleur
Valognes
Montebourg
Tatihou
la Hougue
les Pieux
Bricquebec
Ste Mère Eglise
St Sauveur le Vicomte
Port Bail
la Haye du Puits
Carentan
Isigny
Formigny
Port en Bessin
Rochers du Calvados
Roches de Maisy
Lessay
Periers
St Jean de Daye
Vaubadon
BAYEUX
N.D. de Délivrande
Seulles
Bretteville
CAEN
Orne
Dives
Dozulé
Troarn
Honfleur
Trouville
Touques
Pt L'EVEQUE
LISIEUX
Estrées
Livarot
Vimoutier
Fécamp
Etretat
C. d'Antifer
Epouville
Montivilliers
Harfleur
C. la Heve
LE HAVRE
Seine
COUTANCES
Marigny
ST LÔ
Hauteville la Guichard
Torigny
Caumont
Juvigny
Villers Bocage
Fontenay
Moult
Langannerie
Harcourt
FALAISE
Guibray
Trun
Hambie
Gavray
Tessy
Percy
Mesnil au Zouf
St Sever
Villedieu
Brehal
Granville
Chausey
VIRE
Condé sur Noireau
Pt d'Ouilly
Tinchebray
Flers
Briouze
ARGENTAN
Exmes
Ecouché
le Pin
Nonant
Sartilly
AVRANCHES
Cancale
Tombelene
Mt St Michel
Sourdeval
la Chapelle
MORTAIN
Lonlay
DOMFRONT
la Ferté Macé
Ranes
Mortrée
Seez
Carouges
Ducey
St Hilaire
Pontorson
Dol
St James
le Teilleul
Passais
Bagnolles
Couterne
Mesnil Broust
St Denis
ALENÇON
Sarthe
Antrain
Combourg
Trans
Louvigné
Prez en Pail
Ambrières
le Ribay
FOUGÈRES
St Brice
St Aubin d'Aubigné
St Aubin du Cormier
Liffré
Ernée
MAYENNE
Martigné
Bais
Evron
Fresnay
Beaumont
la Hutte
Sillé le Guillaume
Chateaubourg
VITRÉ
Mayenne
Vilaine
M A Y E N N E
Bonné

Table of Contents

Introduction 4

1. Crosville
The watchman of Cotentin 6

2. Canisy
Help thyself Kergorlay 12

3. Colombières
The gateway to Bessin 18

4. Balleroy
Semper altius 24

5. Fontaine-Henry
The source of history 30

6. Fontaine-Etoupefour
Re-naissance 36

7. Canon
Walls and whispers 42

8. Vendeuvre
Surprises and miniatures 50

9. Le Champ-Versant
A Manor in Auge 58

Le Trou Normand 66

10. Manoir de Saint-Hippolyte
An agricultural manor 68

11. Sassy
Under the watchful eyes of Vatel 74

12. Carrouges
Hunters and hunting 82

13. Bonneville
For the love of a house 92

14. Anet
Diane's Mausoleum 100

15. Fleury-la-Forêt
Patienta et labore 104

16. Manoir de Villers
Manor on the Seine 110

17. Filières
The spice road 118

18. Cany
The Grand Siècle in the Pays de Caux 124

19. Miromesnil
In a nourishing garden 130

Alphabetical Index 138

Practical Guide 140

Map taken from the « Guide du voyageur en Normandie ». Rouen Municipal Library.

Editor: Henri Bancaud
Editorial Coordination: Solenne Lambert
Graphic Design: Brigitte Racine
Printing: Pollina in Luçon (85) - n° L48870

Edilarge SA, Rennes
ISBN: 978-2-7373-4666-8
Legal deposit: January 2009
Editor N°: 5845.01.03.01.09
Printed in France
Find us at www.editionsouestfrance.fr